STORIES FROM JERUSALEM

Adèle Geras

Illustrated by Jael Jordan

Includes
My Grandmother's stories
and
Golden Windows

mammoth

First published in two separate volumes –

My Grandmother's Stories
First published in Great Britain 1990
by Heinemann Young Books
Published 1994 by Mammoth
Text copyright © 1990 Adèle Geras
Illustrations copyright © 1990 Jael Jordan

Golden Windows
First published in Great Britain 1995
by Heinemann Young Books and Mammoth
Text copyright © 1995 Adèle Geras
Illustrations copyright © 1995 Jael Jordan

This new edition first published 1999 by Mammoth
an imprint of Egmont Children's Books Limited
239 Kensington High Street, London W8 6SA

The moral rights of the author and illustrator have been asserted.

ISBN 0 7497 3524 4

10 9 8 7 6 5 4 3 2 1

A CIP catalogue record for this title
is available from the British Library

Printed in Great Britain
by Cox & Wyman Ltd, Reading, Berkshire

Contents

Bavsi's Feast

FIRST of all, let me tell you about my grandmother's kitchen. It was a small, square room with a large sink next to one wall, and a wooden table pushed up to another. Because my

grandmother lived on the third floor of a block of flats, the window in one wall was really a door and opened out on to a small balcony. In summer there would be tall, glass jars lined up at the edge of the balcony; and in the jars tiny, green cucumbers floated in a pale, cloudy liquid, turning into pickles in the sunlight. If only you could taste the dishes that my grandmother cooked: cinnamon cakes, plaited loaves of bread, meats stewed in velvety sauces, fish fried to the colour of gold, soup with matzo dumplings, fragrant with nutmeg; and for the Sabbath, the kugel: a savoury cake made of noodles and eggs, with just a hint of burnt sugar to give it its caramel colour and smoky taste. One of the tasks I enjoyed was helping to mince things. I liked using a carrot to poke whatever we were mincing deep into the silver mouth of the machine clamped to the side of the table. My grandmother liked chopping and talking.

One day, we were making a strudel, cutting up apples to mix with the nuts and the raisins.

"Have you ever thought," she said to me, "what it must be like to be hungry?"

"I'm often hungry," I answered. "I'm hungry now. May I eat the rest of this apple?"

My grandmother laughed. "That's not hunger. That's greed. Let me tell you a story about someone who learned what real hunger meant. He was a merchant, a very rich merchant, who lived a long time ago, in the days of King Solomon."

"Where did he live?"

"He lived in Jerusalem. And he was the meanest, most penny-pinching scoundrel who ever drew breath. He was so mean that he never even married, not wishing to have the additional expense of a wife and children. All over the city people talked of his stinginess. His name became famous. 'Mean as Bavsi', people would say, or sometimes 'evil as Bavsi'. Now one day, a great famine came to the land. The crops had failed and the poor people began to suffer from lack of food. Rich men who were also kind distributed all the contents of their granaries among the starving citizens, but not Bavsi, oh no. Do you know what he did?"

"What?"

"He put huge wooden bars across the doors of his granaries to keep the people out. He cut down on his servants' food and sold his grain at a very high price to those who could manage to scrape together the money. So he grew rich while others starved and suffered. All the stories whispered by those who had good reason to hate him at last reached the ears of King Solomon himself, and when he learned how Bavsi was behaving, he decided to teach the miser a lesson he would not forget."

"What did he do?"

"He sent the Royal Chamberlain to Bavsi's house with an invitation. The merchant was to take dinner with the King, the very next evening. You can imagine how overwhelmed, how excited and how flattered Bavsi was. 'At last!' he said to himself, 'King Solomon realises what a great man I am. How rich! How powerful!' He called his servants at once and set them to work, washing his clothes, and setting out his jewels ready for dinner the next day.

When he woke up in the morning, Bavsi decided not to eat at

all that day. King Solomon's feast was sure to be sumptuous beyond dreams. It would be a pity, therefore, not to do it full justice. So, at six o'clock, Bavsi presented himself at King Solomon's palace. The sun was just setting, and the palace walls were pearly in the apricot light of evening. Bavsi's servants had carried him through the streets on a raised platform, so that the hem of his robe should not become dusty. On every side there were men dressed in rags and white with hunger; children who no longer had any energy left for playing; and women with sunken eyes that were red from weeping. Bavsi saw none of them. He fixed his eyes on Solomon's glittering walls and his mind on the feast that was waiting for him. The truth of the matter was that he was already extremely hungry, not having eaten since the previous night.

In the palace, Bavsi followed the servant who waited at the door to where the Royal Chamberlain was seated, in a wide hall hung with embroideries in the colours of every jewel dug from the earth or found in the depths of the sea.

'Ah, Bavsi,' said the Royal Chamberlain. 'Approach and let me make you welcome! Let me also explain to you how you must behave while you are a guest in the palace. There is, as I'm sure you'll understand, a very rigid form of etiquette on these occasions: certain rules that have to be obeyed.'

'Of course, of course,' Bavsi nodded eagerly. 'I understand perfectly.'

'Very well, then,' said the Royal Chamberlain. 'First of all, you must never, at any time, ask for anything: not from the King, nor from his servants, nor from anyone else. Agreed?'

'Agreed,' said Bavsi. 'What could I possibly need to ask for?' He chuckled happily.

'Secondly,' the Royal Chamberlain continued, 'whatever you may see happening, you must not ask any questions nor utter any complaint.'

'Questions?' said Bavsi. 'Complaints? From me? Never in a million years!'

'And lastly,' said the Royal Chamberlain, 'when King Solomon asks you whether you are enjoying your meal, you must be as lavish as you can be in praising it. Is that understood?'

'It will be my pleasure,' Bavsi smiled. 'My pleasure entirely.'

'Thank you,' said the Royal Chamberlain. 'I do not have to remind you how terrible the King's anger will be if you do not obey these three rules. Now, if you will follow me, dinner is still being prepared. It will be ready in one hour. You are the only guest at this feast. I will ask you to wait here, until the King is ready to dine.'

Bavsi was shown into a small room that looked out on to the courtyard. By now, he was beginning to feel quite faint from hunger, and the very worst thing of all was that there was no door to this small room, and the palace kitchens were just across the courtyard. Every wonderful smell in the world rose up out of that kitchen and drifted through the evening air, straight to where Bavsi was sitting: fragrances that tormented him more than if they had been ghosts from another world."

"What sort of smells?" I asked my grandmother.

"Everything you can think of that's wonderful: bread baking to a golden crust, onions frying, cinnamon lingering in the air, meat roasting in aromatic oils, spices being pounded in stone jars, rose petals being steeped in water, ready to be crystallised in sugar – every good smell that there could be in a kitchen was there that night. I can almost find it in my heart to feel sorry for Bavsi, but not quite. He was only a little sorry for himself, for he comforted himself with the thought that soon, very soon, he would be eating alone with the great King and conversing with the wisest man in all the world. It was worth waiting for.

At last, the moment arrived and Bavsi was led into the room in which King Solomon was waiting for him, lying on cushions made of silk and embroidered with threads of silver.

'Sit, Bavsi,' said King Solomon, 'and let us eat.' Bavsi sat, and a servant carried in a bowl of soup like liquid gold and set it before King Solomon. Another servant followed with a bowl which he set in front of Bavsi, but before the merchant could pick up his spoon, a third servant took Bavsi's bowl and carried it away, leaving the unfortunate creature holding his spoon up in the air. He was just about to say something when he remembered his promise to the Royal Chamberlain, so he smiled at the King while the devils of hunger began to move around in his stomach, so that he felt pain and nausea and dizziness as he watched Solomon smacking his lips with every mouthful.

After the soup came a whole fish baked in vine leaves and laid on a bed of rice. Then came roasted meats. Then cakes dripping with honey and studded with nuts, and velvety fruits fragrant with luscious juices, and with each course the same thing happened: the food was taken away from Bavsi before he had time to touch it. Bavsi felt completely bewildered.

'How are you enjoying your meal?' King Solomon asked. And Bavsi, remembering his promise said, 'It is the most wondrous meal I have ever eaten.'

Meanwhile, he was thinking: not long now. Soon this torment will be over. I will leave the palace and return to my own house and eat my food. It may be plain, but it is food. Soon, soon I will be gone from here.

But Bavsi had reckoned without King Solomon.

'Stay and listen to some music,' the King said, and Bavsi had to stay, for the ruler's word was law.

When the musicians had left, and Bavsi rose to go, King Solomon said, 'You must stay the night. It is far too late for you to go home. The servants will show you to your bedchamber.'

Bavsi did not sleep at all. His hunger was gnawing at him, just as though a large rat had taken up residence in his stomach, and it was not only hunger that was troubling him.

'Why' he said to himself, 'has the King done this to me? He has deliberately kept all food and drink from me. It must be a punishment. He must be teaching me something. What have I learned? Only the meaning of real hunger, so that must be what King Solomon intended.'

When Bavsi arrived at his own house the next morning, he threw open his granary doors and distributed his corn to the poor, and never again sold food to the starving people to make a profit for himself. There. Now you can have a piece of apple.''

The Faces of the Czar

THE cupboard in my grandmother's bedroom was big and
brown, with a long mirror set into its central panel. If you
opened the cupboard doors, there were shelves upon shelves
filled with sheets and pillowcases, towels and tablecloths, and
even some containing folded underwear and lots of rolled-up
brown balls of stockings. Right at the bottom there was a

drawer, and it was in this drawer that the button-box was kept. It was made of tin: a dull, silvery colour. I don't know what used to be kept in it, nor what it had held when it first came into the house; but now it was full of buttons. When I took it out of the drawer and moved it around in my hands, all the buttons made a sushy-rattly sound as they moved against the metal sides of the box. I liked spilling them on to the black and yellow tiles of the bedroom floor, where I arranged them in groups according to size, or colour, or beauty, or spread them out in huge patterns all around me. Sometimes, my cousins and I used the buttons as pretend money. Silver ones were the most valuable of all, and there were six buttons (from a dress that had once belonged to my aunt in America) which had the face of a man with a beard and a crown scratched on to them.

"Such a face," my grandmother said, "could only belong to a Czar. Do you know what a Czar was?"

I shook my head.

"A Czar was a Russian emperor, the kind of ruler whose very lightest word was law, the kind of ruler before whom everyone trembled, and more especially the poor peasant, trying to scratch a bare living out of a tiny patch of ground. And of course, as well as being powerful, and wicked more often than not, Czars, like all other rulers, were in the habit of having little pictures of themselves stamped on to every coin in the kingdom. All this talk of Czars reminds me of the story of Frankel the farmer. Have I told you about him before?"

"No, never," I said. "Tell me about him now."

"So put all the buttons back in the box and I'll begin."

"Are they all in? Good. Now, long ago, in a very far away and neglected corner of Russia, about a day's ride from the Czar's Summer Palace, there lived a farmer called Frankel. On this particular day that I'm telling you of, Frankel was happily occupied digging up turnips in what he called his field, but which in truth was a piece of land about the size of a tablecloth. He was content. The sun was shining for once, the turnips had all turned out well, large and pleasantly mauve and white in colour, and their leaves were so prettily green and feathery that Frankel sang as he worked. He was absorbed in his labours, so that he hardly noticed the horseman drawing nearer and nearer, until the noise of the hoof-beats on the dry earth of the road made him look up. What he saw made him drop his spade in amazement. It was the Czar. Frankel bowed deeply.

'Do not be surprised, my friend,' said the Czar. 'Often, when I'm sick to death of court councils and endless feasts, I saddle my horse and go riding about my kingdom, talking to my subjects. I am very interested to observe that although the hair on your head is grey, the hairs of your beard are still black. It's something I've often noticed in people before, and yet no one seems to know the reason for it.'

'O, mighty Czar,' Frankel replied (reasoning that he couldn't possibly be too polite to a Czar), 'I am only a poor Jewish farmer, but the reason is this. The hairs on my head started growing when I was born. Those on my chin only started growing when I was thirteen years old, after the Bar Mitzvah ceremony at which I became a man. Therefore, the hairs on my chin are much younger and not yet grey.'

'Amazing!' said the Czar. 'How simple and yet how logical! I'm overjoyed to have discovered the answer to a question that has long been puzzling me. Now, I beg of you, my friend, tell no one else what you have told me. Let it remain a secret between us. Do you agree?'

'I will only reveal our secret after I have seen your face a hundred times, Sire,' said Frankel. So the Czar set off on his horse, chuckling to himself, and Frankel continued digging up his turnips.

When the Czar arrived at the Palace, he asked all his advisers to gather round.

'Here,' he said 'is a question. Why does the hair on the head grow grey before the hair of the beard? Whoever can answer that question for me will be promoted to the position of Chief Adviser to the Czar, and will sit in a specially-fashioned silver throne studded with lumps of amber the size of small onions.'

All the advisers scurried about, asking everyone they met, consulting books too heavy to be carried, and working out every possibility on scrolls of paper a yard long. This went on for weeks. Finally, two of the chancellors discussed the matter.

'I remember,' said one, 'that on the day the Czar asked us the question, he had come back from a ride to the Western Territory. Perhaps he found the answer there. If we ride in the same direction, maybe we'll come across it too.'

Thus it happened that one rainy day as Frankel was listening sadly to the sucking noises made by his boots entering and leaving the mud, two horsemen galloped up to where he was standing.

'Good day to you, farmer,' said one of the horsemen. 'We are advisers to the Czar, and we have reason to think that the Czar may have ridden this way a few weeks ago.'

'He did,' Frankel agreed. 'And now, here you are. This part of the world hasn't ever been quite so busy. A person hardly has the leisure to tend his property.'

'But did you tell the Czar why it is that the hair on the head turns grey before the hair of the beard?'

'I did, but I'm not at liberty to tell you gentlemen.'

The chancellors sighed. 'Is there nothing we can do to persuade you to change your mind?'

Frankel considered. 'One hundred silver roubles will change my mind instantly.'

'Then take these, my friend,' said one of the chancellors, 'and tell us the answer to the riddle.'

Frankel took the coins, sat down in the road, and spread the coins out on his lap to count them. When he had finished, he told the Czar's advisers exactly what he had told the Czar. The men sprang into their saddles and left for the Palace at a gallop, feeling very pleased with themselves, but not as pleased as Frankel, who had suddenly acquired wealth.

The trouble only began when they came to the Czar and told him the answer.

'How can you possibly know this?' shouted the Czar.

'We met a Jewish farmer called Frankel on the road,' they said, 'and he told us.'

'And he undertook to say nothing, the scoundrel!' The Czar stamped his foot and sent for his Chief of Police. 'Go to the farm of the Jew, Frankel, and bring him here at once. Also, alert the firing squad. This will be Frankel's last day on earth.'

Well, eventually the Police brought Frankel to see the Czar.

'What have you to say for yourself, you wretch?' yelled the Czar. 'Did you not promise me that you would not reveal the secret you told me?'

'I said,' Frankel whispered, 'that I would only reveal it after I had seen your face a hundred times.'

'But this is only the second time you have seen me, you worm! What have you to say for yourself before I have you shot?'

'Forgive me, Czar,' said Frankel, and he took out the bag containing the hundred silver roubles which the chancellors had given him. 'Here are one hundred coins. I have looked at every one. Therefore, I'm sure you will agree, I have seen your face one hundred times.'

The Czar was stunned, full of admiration for Frankel's sharp wits.

'I shall get rid of all my advisers and appoint you instead,' he chuckled. 'You shall sit at my left hand on a silver throne studded with amber lumps the size of small onions. You shall want for nothing, my friend.'

And so Frankel lived to a ripe old age, and became the richest and most powerful man in Russia, next only to the Czar himself."

The Golden Shoes

THERE were other cupboards in my grandmother's flat, as well as the big brown one in her bedroom. In the room where only the grandest of guests was entertained, there was a long, blue sofa and next to it, a glass-fronted cabinet full of books. I was allowed to turn the brass key and open the doors, and take out some of the books.

"The ones on the top shelf are too heavy for you," my grandmother used to say, and I never minded because they looked dark and stiff in their leather covers, and the pages crackled as they turned, as though they might break if you touched them. I used to take out the smaller books on the lower shelves, and sniff the pages. I knew the little black marks on the paper were words because sometimes my grandmother would read a story aloud to me, but mainly I liked the smell. Every book has a special fragrance: a mixture of ink and glue and a distant memory of the trees that the paper was made from, but I've never found other books that smelled as good as those that lived behind glass in the cabinet next to the long sofa.

In the dining-room, a sideboard took up most of one wall. On top of the sideboard lived two brass bowls filled with fruit. Under the bowls there were round lace mats which my aunt Sara had crocheted from silky threads. At the bottom of the sideboard, there were three sets of wooden doors for me to open. One cupboard I closed immediately: there was nothing in it but glasses — wine glasses with twisted stems, plain water-glasses, tiny little glasses which no one ever used, and a brand-new set of tumblers, which had pictures of red flowers painted all round the tops. My aunts, Miriam and Dina, had sent them all the way from America. The next cupboard held the silver box full of spices, which my grandmother used to let me sniff at every Saturday evening as she said the prayers for the beginning of another week. There were pictures and patterns on every side of the box, cut into the silver so that you could go over the long, curly beards of the men with your fingertips, or follow the outlines of the birds and animals. Also in this cupboard lived the candlesticks (brass ones for every day and silver ones for special occasions), the embroidered cloths for covering up the plaited loaves of Sabbath bread, a few spare velvet skull-caps (in case visitors forgot to bring theirs when they came to a Sabbath dinner), and some square prayer books whose pages were rimmed with gold paint.

The last cupboard of all was the best. In it, my grandmother kept boxes of crystallized fruit, Turkish delight and chocolate. She wrapped the boxes up in newspaper, very carefully, but I knew what was hidden and so did my cousins. We'd open the door and put our noses in, and breathe the velvety chocolate smell, but no one ever dared to steal from this cupboard because my grandmother always knew exactly what she'd wrapped up, and how much of everything was left over after she'd distributed the day's treat. This always happened after dinner.

"Go to the cupboard," she'd say to me, "and bring me the flat parcel next to the wall." Or "Bring me the little parcel on the right hand side at the back," and I would bring it, and wait to see what would be unwrapped. The grown-ups would drink their lemon tea (from the American glasses, which fitted into little plastic holders, so that you could pick them up without burning yourself) and we would eat flat rectangles of chocolate on which a word had been stamped in lovely, curly letters. My grandmother read it out to me.

"That says 'Splendide'," she nodded wisely. "It's the French word for splendid." I thought that the word described the chocolate very well.

The best cupboard of all was in the bedroom and it wasn't really a cupboard at all, just a small set of shelves with a curtain hanging on a wire that you could pull across to hide the rows and rows of shoes that were kept there. Most of the shoes belonged to my aunt Sara.

"She has such small feet," my grandmother used to say to me. "Not much bigger than yours. And how she loves to buy shoes!"

Whenever I looked on the shelves, all the buckles and pointed toes and dainty heels, all the different colours of the leather: brown and black and white and pink seemed to say to me, try us on . . . don't be afraid. I used to pick out a pair I thought looked pretty, and put my bare feet into them. Then I would walk up and down, making sure to stay in front of the mirror so that I could see myself being a lady. The hard little heels rang on the black and yellow tiles, and up and down I went, glancing over my shoulder as I walked away from the mirror to see if I looked more like a lady from the back than from the front.

"You remind me," my grandmother said to me one day when I had chosen to put on a pair of silver sandals, "of the story of the Wisest Man in Chelm."

"Where's Chelm?" I said. "And who was the wisest man? And why do I remind you of him?"

"Take the silver sandals off and put them away and I'll tell you."

I put the sandals back on the shelf, pulled the curtain carefully across, hiding the beautiful shoes, and went to sit beside my grandmother on the bed.

"Chelm," she said, "is a small town which, they say, is right in the middle of Poland. Or perhaps it's Hungary. Because it isn't a real place, because you can't find it on any map, that means you can put it anywhere you like."

I smiled. "It's a magic place. It's somewhere you've made up."

"Me? I couldn't make up such a place if I live to be a hundred and twenty," said my grandmother. "Always, for as long as I can remember, there have been stories told about the people of Chelm and believe me, there's nothing magic about them. On the contrary, every single person who ever lived in the town of Chelm was a fool."

"Not one clever person in the whole town?" I asked.

"Not one. Fools, dolts, idiots, and simpletons, from the teacher to the butcher, from the carpenter to the baker. And not only them, their wives and children too. They were fools as well."

"Were they happy?"

"They were as happy and as unhappy as anyone else, I suppose, but they had their own ways of solving problems."

"Did they have a problem about shoes?"

"Not about shoes, not exactly. What happened, happened like this. One day, all the people of Chelm decided that there should be a Council of Wise Men to look after the day-to-day business of the town. Ten people were chosen to be the Council, and then those ten people chose the cleverest among them to be the Chief Sage."

"But were they really clever?" I asked.

"No, they were fools. Everyone in Chelm is a fool, whether his name is Chief Sage or not. You must remember that."

"I will. What happened next?"

"The Council of Wise Men decided that the Chief Sage should wear a special pair of golden shoes whenever he walked about the town, so that everyone would recognise him and see that he *was* the Chief Sage and not just an ordinary citizen. The shoemaker made a beautiful pair of sparkling golden shoes, and the Chief Sage put them on at once and went walking about the town. Unfortunately, it had been raining the night before and the streets were deep in mud. The Chief Sage had hardly taken twenty steps before his beautiful shoes were covered in mud and not the tiniest speck of gold could be seen. 'This will never do,' he said to the Council of Wise Men. 'No one could see my gold shoes because of the mud. What is the solution to the problem?' The Council of Wise Men sat up all night debating the matter, and by morning they had found the answer: the shoemaker would make a pair of ordinary brown boots, which the Chief Sage could slip on over his golden shoes, thus keeping the mud away from their glittering surface. Oh, the Council of Wise Men was delighted with this solution, and so was the Chief Sage, and he stepped out happily in his golden shoes with the brown leather boots on over the top. To his amazement, however, not one single citizen of Chelm recognised him while he was walking through the town.

'No one recognised me!' he cried to the Council of Wise Men. 'They couldn't see the golden shoes because of the brown boots covering them up!'

'Aah!' sighed the Council of Wise Men. 'How clever of you to have worked that out! It's not for nothing we elected you to be our Chief Sage!' They sighed again. 'But what is to be done?'

One of the Council had a moment of inspiration. 'I know!' he cried. 'Let the shoemaker cut a pattern of small holes along the side of the brown boots, and right across the toes, and then the golden shoes will be visible through the holes!'

Murmurs of 'Brilliant!' and 'Wonderful!' rippled round the Council Chamber. The brown boots were taken to the shoemaker and he punched a pattern of small, star-shaped holes all over the leather. The Chief Sage put them on as soon as they were ready, and set off for another walk around the town . . . but again the streets were muddy, and the mud came through the holes and hid the golden shoes.

No one recognised the Chief Sage and everyone in the Council of Wise Men was in despair. They discussed the problem for many days and many nights, and at last arrived at a perfect solution. Now, if you go to Chelm and walk around, you will know at once who the wisest man in the whole town is. It's quite clear. He's the one who walks about with a pair of golden shoes on his hands, wearing them as though they were gloves!"

I laughed and said, "Tell me another story about Chelm. Are there any more stories?"

"There are many," said my grandmother. "I'll tell you an-other one another day."

"No, now. Please now. Just a very little story."

"Like the one about the bread and butter?"

"Is that a little story?"

"It's a very small story indeed."

"Then tell it."

"Very well," said my grandmother. "Two men of science in Chelm were discussing a very interesting question. When you drop a piece of bread and butter on the floor, does it always fall with the buttery side down?

Yankel said, 'Yes, it always does.'

Mandel said, 'No, it only falls like that sometimes.'

'I will prove it to you,' Yankel said. 'I will butter a slice of bread and drop it on the floor, and you will see what you will see!'

He buttered a slice of bread and dropped it on the floor. It fell with the dry side down and the buttery side up.

'You see . . .' said Mandel triumphantly, 'I was right. It fell with the buttery side up.'

'Nonsense,' said Yankel. 'It was my fault. I made a mistake. I buttered the wrong side, that's all!'"

The Tablecloth

OUTSIDE the front door of my grandmother's flat there was a flight of stairs leading to the roof: a wide, flat area bordered by a stone parapet where all the families in the building used to hang their washing. If you went up on laundry day, the whole roof was aflutter with damp sheets and tablecloths, flapping shirts and blouses, scarves like flags waving, flocks of white handkerchiefs like doves, and here and there, strange and wonderful garments which made my cousins and me laugh behind my grandmother's back: Mrs Sirkis's huge lace-edged bloomers, and the long, skinny, striped socks belonging to the dentist who lived on the first floor. The clothes on the washing-line smelled strongly of pale yellow soap, and were held on the line by wooden clothes-pegs that had been bleached pale grey by the sun. My grandmother used to bring the wet clothes up to the roof in a big tin tub. This tub had a handle on each side, and once the clothes were pegged out, it was light enough for me to hold on to one of the handles and help my grandmother carry it downstairs again.

The roof seemed very high up to me. There were days when it frightened me to look over the parapet and down, down, down into the street. Far below us, I could see the door to Genzel's shop, and although the things that people were buying were in their baskets as they came out, my grandmother knew exactly what everyone had gone to the shop for.

"There's Mrs Rakov buying herrings," she'd say. "She is making chopped herring tonight. Look, there's Mr Lapidas, he's bought some bagels and cream cheese . . . that's what he likes for his lunch, bagels and cheese . . . Mrs Blumberg needs onions . . . there were none in her kitchen yesterday . . . this I saw with my own eyes . . ." and so on.

I liked going to Genzel's shop. It was so near the flat that sometimes my grandmother would put money in my hand and send me down there for something: a few grams of cheese or a packet of tea. I followed the stairs, round and round and round from the third floor to the street, quite by myself, and then I carefully crossed over the little side road and went into the dark treasure-cave of Genzel's shop. I wasn't frightened because I knew that my grandmother was watching me from the balcony, and I always waved at her from the corner. Genzel's shelves were filled with tins and boxes, and the small room smelled of soap and salt and cheese and wax, the silver herrings bobbing in the big, brown barrel, the shiny black olives floating in inky water, and the round yellow cheeses on the counter. Sacks of flour stood open by the entrance, and there were sweets in glass jars near the drawer where Mrs Genzel kept her money. Strings of onions hung from the ceiling, and tall people went into the shop with their heads bent. Genzel was thin and wore a dusty black jacket. Mrs Genzel was fat and if you didn't watch out, she'd pinch your cheek between her thumb and forefinger, muttering endearments, or even give you a fishy-smelling kiss. I used to ask for whatever I wanted and Genzel would get it for me, wrap it in newspaper and put it in my basket, and take my money and give me change. Mrs Genzel would give me a wonderful sweet like a marble that tasted of aniseed and changed colour as I sucked it.

My cousin Danny and I had a special game that we used to play on the roof. We'd collected lots of broken clothes-pegs and hidden the tiny pieces of wood under a bucket. We used to wait until a man wearing a hat went past, far, far below us in the street, and then we'd throw a piece of peg over the parapet and lean over to see whether it had landed in the man's hat, or at least near enough to make him look up. If anyone *did* look up, we used to crouch down where we couldn't be seen and laugh and laugh.

One day in spring, as I was looking over the edge, waiting for my grandmother to finish hanging out the washing, I saw something astonishing.

"Come quickly and look," I said to my grandmother. "There's a man walking past with an animal curled round his head . . . it must be asleep."

My grandmother looked. "Silly girl! Haven't you seen a streimel before?"

"What's a streimel?"

"A hat with fur all round the crown."

"Oh . . . well, maybe I have seen one . . . but it looks different from up here. Not like a fur hat at all. Just like a cat wrapped round the man's head. Why is he wearing a fur hat on such a warm day?"

"Because it's a kind of uniform. It shows that that man is very religious. He spends most of his days studying the scriptures. His mind, you see, is on higher things than hats, or whether he's feeling too warm. He may even," said my grandmother, "be a rabbi. You know what a rabbi is, don't you?"

"Oh, yes," I said. "He takes services in the synagogue."

"And that's not all he does," said my grandmother. "Rabbis have to be especially clever men, not only because they are dealing with God's work all day long, but also because they have to give advice, settle arguments, help everyone to live together peacefully . . . it's a difficult job, I can tell you. Just like being in charge of an enormous family. Of course, the cleverest rabbi I ever knew was Rabbi Samuels, who lived down there . . ." She pointed to a spot near the horizon, and I craned my head to see, fully expecting Rabbi Samuels to be visible, perhaps even to be waving at us. "He's dead now, poor man," my grandmother continued, "but he was the cleverest rabbi who ever lived, and do you know why?"

"Why?"

"Because he married a clever woman. Her name was Rivka, and while he studied the holy texts and communicated with the Almighty, she looked and listened and went to the shop and the market and talked to everyone and knew everything, which meant that she could give the Rabbi excellent advice from time to time. Oh, the Rabbi acquired such a reputation for cleverness, thanks to her, people came from miles around to ask him about their problems . . . as they did in the matter of the tablecloth."

"Tell me the story of the tablecloth," I said.

My grandmother sat down on the upturned tin tub, and began.

"Long ago, when I was a little girl, there were no modern buildings like this one, with flats one on top of another. No, the people lived in rooms arranged around four sides of a courtyard. In our courtyard, we used to sit outside in summer on chairs taken from the dining room. There were big flowerpots with geraniums growing in them, and sometimes a family would put a rabbit hutch in the courtyard and all the children would come and try to stroke the rabbit through the wire. The courtyard was also the place where washing was hung out to dry. On one side of the building lived a woman called Pnina with her family; and on the other side, directly opposite, lived a women called Malka with her husband and children. Now Pnina's name means 'pearl' and truly, she was a pearl among women: kind and thoughtful and loving and friendly. Malka's name means 'queen', and that is what she felt she should have been. But of course, she was not a queen, so her whole life was spoiled by envying others their good fortune, and by moaning constantly about her dreadful luck. No one liked her. Even her own family found her tiring and annoying, which naturally gave her even more to complain about . . . and so life went on for some time.

Now Malka thought everyone better off than herself, but Pnina aroused in her feelings of desperate envy. On Thursdays, when Pnina pinned out her newly-washed tablecloth, ready for the Sabbath, Malka's heart folded itself into little pleats of anguish, for the tablecloth was something out of a dream, and it was Pnina's and not hers."

"What was it like?" I wanted to know.

"Oh, huge and white and shining. When the wind sprang up behind it and made it billow out over the courtyard, it was as though a beautiful white swan had spread its wings, or as though a tall ship had sailed into the courtyard. All over the white linen there were damasked patterns of whiter lilies and roses that caught the light and glowed like satin. Round the sides there were tiny squares of drawn threadwork, and the cloth was edged with finest lace . . . oh, it was something to see. Now, let me continue with the story. Everyone knew that the cloth had been sent to Pnina when she was married, by a rich uncle who lived in Warsaw. We all knew the tablecloth well. That's what made Malka's behaviour all the more astonishing . . ."

"Tell me . . ."

"I'm telling you. One day, Pnina must have been in a hurry to hang out the washing, because when the wind started to blow, it lifted the pegs off the line and sent the tablecloth flying right over to the far side of the courtyard, where it landed outside Malka's kitchen door. Now Malka had been filling partly-cooked cabbage-leaves with spoonfuls of rice and fried onions and carrots and little pieces of meat, and rolling them up into neat, pale green parcels, and putting them into the pot, ready to cover with water and lemon juice . . . They had to cook slowly, slowly, for the evening meal. When she glanced out of the window and saw the tablecloth, she did not hesitate for a moment. She washed her hands, and stepping out into the courtyard, she picked up the tablecloth, shook it out in full view of everyone, and began to fold it. It was then that Pnina noticed what had happened. She came running across to where Malka was standing.

'Oh, Malka,' she said, 'thank you for catching my tablecloth.

The wind must have blown it over here . . . and thank you for folding it so well.'

Malka gave a sugary smile. 'I'm afraid you're mistaken. This is *my* tablecloth. It does look rather like the one you show off to us every day almost, but alas, this cloth is mine.'

'No,' Pnina went white. 'It's mine . . . it was a wedding present from my uncle in Warsaw. I know it as well as I know my own children's faces.'

Malka laughed. 'You are not the only one with relations. I have an aunt in Cracow. She sent me the tablecloth. You are surely not saying that Cracow tablecloths are inferior to Warsaw tablecloths?'

'No, no . . .' Pnina was nearly weeping. 'I am only saying that that is *my* tablecloth.'

'And I am saying it's mine.'

'But it isn't . . .'

'It is . . .'

'It isn't . . .'

A crowd of neighbours gathered round the two women. Matters could have gone on like this for hours, but then someone shouted out: 'Go to Rabbi Samuels. Let him decide whose tablecloth it is.'

'A good idea,' said all the neighbours.

So Malka and Pnina set off for Rabbi Samuel's house, with Malka still clutching the tablecloth to her rather ample bosom.

The Rabbi sat in his chair, next to the table and listened to the two women telling their stories. The Rabbi's wife, Rivka, was in the kitchen, making chopped liver, mashing the meat up with chicken fat and an onion very finely chopped, and adding a little bit of parsley and salt and pepper. This task, however, did not prevent her from hearing every word that Pnina and Malka were saying. She always left the kitchen door open. Glancing at her husband in his chair, and observing the manner in which he was stroking his beard, Rivka realised that the Rabbi had no immediate solution to the problem.

'Beloved,' she called from the kitchen, 'would you be good enough to come here for one moment?'

'Excuse me, ladies,' said the Rabbi, glad of the opportunity to consult his wife. He left Pnina and Malka standing next to his chair, while he went into the kitchen, taking the tablecloth with him. Pnina and Malka leaned forward to hear what the Rabbi was saying to his wife, but at first they heard only whisperings. Then in Rivka's voice came these words, which Pnina and Malka both heard quite clearly.

'What a magnificent tablecloth! Such a pity about this tiny, tiny stain of red wine here in this corner.'

'Yes,' the Rabbi could be heard saying. 'A great shame indeed!'

When the Rabbi came out of the kitchen, he was smiling.

'Now, ladies, it has, luckily, been very easy for me to make a decision in this matter. Which of you has a tablecloth with a small pink wine stain in one corner?'

Malka's eyes sparkled. 'Oh, that's me! Four Sabbaths ago, my little boy, Eliezer, spilled the wine. Even though I put salt on it at once, a pink stain still remains. There is nothing I can do about it. It just won't come out.'

'And what have you to say to that, Pnina?' asked the Rabbi. 'Is she telling the truth?'

'Yes,' said Pnina, 'she must be, because of one thing I am quite certain: there were no wine stains on my tablecloth. My tablecloth is white all over.'

With a wide sweep of his arms like a fisherman casting a net over water, the Rabbi spread the cloth out for Pnina and Malka to see.

'This, then, must be Pnina's cloth,' he said, smiling 'because as you can see, both of you, there is no stain of any kind anywhere upon it.'

Pnina took her property lovingly back into her arms, and thanked the Rabbi. Malka was disgraced, and although she was seething with rage at the Rabbi's trick, there was nothing at all she could say. Her stuffed cabbage had nearly boiled dry by the time she returned to her kitchen. 'Nothing ever goes right for me,' she sighed as she ate her food.

Pnina continued to serve her Sabbath dinner on the beautiful tablecloth till the day she died. And thanks to his wife's quick thinking, Rabbi Samuels became known throughout the neighbourhood as the wisest of men."

A Tangle of Wools

IN the dining-room of my grandmother's flat, as well as a large table, eight wooden chairs and the sideboard, there was a bed pushed up against one wall. This was only used as a bed at night. During the day it was covered with a dark cloth and became a divan for people to sit on. My grandmother put cushions on it, to make it look more comfortable. On the wall beside it hung two of the things I liked best in the world. First, and highest up the wall, so high that I couldn't touch it even if I stood on the bed, was a very large photograph of an aunt of mine who had died before I was born. This photograph showed a dark-haired lady in a lacy blouse with a very high collar. I liked her because she looked beautiful and gentle, and because I shared her name. There she was, every day, leaning on her hand and looking out at everyone from inside the square made by the heavy black wood of the frame around her portrait. Below this picture hung the Cross Stitch Mountains. No one else called them that, it was my name for them. Everyone else called them 'The Tapestry'. The Cross Stitch Mountains covered almost the whole wall behind the bed, and when I stood next to it, my head only came about half-way up the pattern. I never really knew who embroidered all the millions and millions of cross-stitches on to the canvas, in all those colours: red and yellow and orange and black and green. The stitches gathered themselves together into shapes like zigzagging peaks of mountains. First, there'd be a small line of pointed black triangles, then bigger green ones on top of them, then orange, then blue, then green again . . . All the way up the canvas: never-ending ranges of mountains piled up, one on top of another. I used to think that perhaps my dead aunt had made it and that was why it hung below her picture, but my grandmother told me once that all her daughters, even my mother, had taken their turn and added their own stitches to the pattern.

"You should have seen us," she would say to me "in the days when your mother was a girl! There was wool all over this house. It reminds me of the story of the 'plonter'."

"What's that? What's a 'plonter'?"

"A 'plonter' is a mess of tangled wools, all bundled up together in a basket."

"Is there a story about that?" I asked.

"Certainly," said my grandmother. "There is a story about almost everything . . . now let me see . . . where shall I begin? You know, don't you, that in the olden days . . . well, not really such olden days, because it happened to me . . . parents chose a suitable husband or wife for their child. They would look around at the children of other families whom they knew, and think: perhaps young Selig, or Ruth, will be a good husband or wife for our child . . . and then a matchmaker would run between the two families arranging meetings and seeing if the two young people were suitable for each other."

"What happened if you didn't like the person your parents chose for you?" I asked.

"Well then of course, the wedding couldn't be arranged and the whole business would start all over again. But the first thing that had to happen was that the parents had to choose. And how? How does one choose between one girl and another?"

"How?" I wanted to know.

"Let me tell you the story of Hannah and Reuben and you'll see. They were a happy couple, living in perfect harmony with their neighbours and their children. Hannah was the best of women, but she did have one failing. Her basket of wools resembled a nest of snakes. Every thread was twisted and knotted and tangled in with its neighbours, and each time poor Hannah wished to embark upon a piece of darning, or start to knit a sock for her husband, she would be nearly weeping with frustration as she tried to separate off one colour from another. It wasn't a basket of wools at all. What it was, was a 'plonter'. Well, Hannah and Reuben had a son, and it was time for this son to settle down with a wife. Hannah and Reuben employed a matchmaker to find him a suitable bride. Now this was all very good and fine for Hannah and Reuben and the matchmaker, who spent many a pleasant afternoon together, discussing the qualities of every single young lady of their acquaintance over cups of tea and biscuits flavoured with almond essence and sprinkled with sugar. But Hannah and Reuben's son – let us call him Jacob – had other ideas. He wanted to marry his friend Rachel. They had grown up together and they loved each other.

One day, Jacob went to see his mother and father. They were alone, for once. He brought Rachel with him.

'Father, Mother, I would like you to know,' said Jacob 'that I wish to marry Rachel.'

"What did they say?" I asked. "Did they let him?"

"I'm glad," said my grandmother "that you have never heard an argument such as went on there, in that house! There were shoutings, and cryings, and curses and threats and pleas, backwards and forwards and up and down for hours. Poor Rachel, forgotten during all this commotion between the parents and their child, sat at the table with Hannah's basket of wools in front of her. And as the storms of words and tears flew around her head, she began to unpick the knots in the wool, sort out one colour from another, untwist strands that had been twisted together for longer than anyone could remember, and wind the different colours into little skeins, shaped like small figures-of-eight. During a lull in the argument, Hannah glanced at her basket and saw that now her wools were lying curled up inside it in neat circles, all the colours singing out one after the other, distinct and beautiful, like summer flowers gathered in a vase.

'Reuben,' she said to her husband, 'I think we may have underestimated Rachel. Look at my wool basket.'

'You, my dear Hannah,' said Reuben 'never had a wool basket. You had a mess. A 'plonter'. *That* is what I call a wool basket. Any woman who can sort out a tangle like the one created by my beloved wife with her threads, is capable of great feats of patience and perseverance. Let this be a lesson to us, Hannah my dear, not to overlook a treasure that is under our noses simply because we are used to it. Rachel my dear, we would be honoured if you would consider marrying our son.''

"So did they marry and live happily ever after?" I asked. My grandmother laughed. "They married. Ever after I don't know about, but what I do know is that matchmakers, ever since that day, used to take a messy bundle of wools with them, and test out prospective brides. Any young woman who grew impatient and thrust the bundle from her in disgust had a couple of black marks written up against her name."

While my grandmother was telling me this story, I had been trying to make my own cross-stitches on a small piece of canvas. I was using wool and a long, silver needle, nearly as long as one of my fingers. I wanted my stitches to make the shape of a house, but when I looked down at my work, it didn't look like a house at all. Some of the walls were crooked and bulged outwards.

"Look," I said, almost crying, "it's horrible. It's not what it's supposed to be at all."

My grandmother looked. Then she took the work out of my hands and put it on the table.

"Let me tell you about the diamond," she said.

"Which diamond?"

"This was the largest and purest diamond in the world. It belonged to a great and powerful king. Now one day, a dreadful accident happened and the diamond was found to have a deep scratch in it. The king was more upset than he had ever been in his life. His perfect diamond was ruined for ever. What was he to do?"

"What *did* he do?"

"He asked every jeweller he knew whether the gem could be polished to remove the scratch, and they were all agreed that it could not be done. The king was heartbroken, until one day, a jeweller arrived at the court from a far country, and asked to see the diamond.

'Give the jewel to me for a week,' said the stranger, 'and I will return it more beautiful than it was before.' Well, of course the king was overjoyed, but he couldn't allow the diamond out of his palace. Therefore he set the man to work in one of the rooms next to his own throne-room, with two guards standing outside the door. When the week was over, the jeweller showed the king what he had done. Using the deep scratch on the diamond to form the stem, he had carved a rose growing out of it, complete with leaves and petals and little rosebuds around it . . . all clearly cut into the jewel.

'You will be richly rewarded,' said the king 'for improving on perfection.'

'The reward should not be for that,' answered the jeweller. 'But for taking a fault and transforming it into a virtue.'"

"I like the story," I said to my grandmother, "but what about my house?"

"It doesn't look like a house," said my grandmother. "It looks more like a face . . . so we'll turn the roof into a hat, and the windows into eyes, and we'll add a mouth smiling . . . and there you are."

And that is what we did.

Saving the Pennies

I N my grandmother's bedroom, in the corner opposite the big brown cupboard, there stood an enormous wooden chest. The lid was too heavy for me to lift by myself, and my grandmother often said to me, "Never lift the lid of this chest on your own. If it were to fall on your fingers . . ." She would

shake her head then, as though she couldn't bear even to think of it. I was not interested in the contents of the chest. It was full of pillows and sheets and blankets and rolled-up quilts in embroidered white quilt-covers.

"Why do we take all the pillows and blankets and put them away in the chest every morning?" I wanted to know. "It means that we have to make the beds again every night."

"It's not such a terrible thing, to make a bed," said my grandmother. "If we left the beds all ready, the whole flat would look like a big dormitory. When my children were small, and my mother was still alive . . . ah, she was a wonderful woman. Have I ever told you about her?"

"Tell me again."

"We called her the Bobbeh. It means 'Grandmother'. Towards the end of her life, she became quite blind, but making all the beds at night, every night, was a task that she enjoyed. It took a long time . . . I had nine living children, remember. The Bobbeh used to take each pillow out of the chest and sniff it carefully. 'This one's Leah's,' she would say. 'This is Matilda's . . . and Sara's and Reuben's' and so on, sniffing every single one and putting it on the right bed. And she never, never made a mistake."

"Never?"

"Never. She was a remarkable woman."

Sometimes my grandmother wanted to clean the floor behind the chest, and Danny and I would help her pile all the bed linen on to one of the beds, and push the chest away from the corner. When it was empty, while my grandmother was busy cleaning the place where it had stood, Danny and I would climb into it and pretend it was a big brown boat that we were sailing across dangerous seas.

"If this chest had wheels," Danny said to my grandmother, "you could push us all over the room . . . all over the flat. Then it really *would* be like a boat."

"Wheels on a chest!" said my grandmother. "That's all I need . . . a chance to spend my days pushing little children across the floor . . . it's a very good thing that chests are absolutely forbidden to have wheels."

"Forbidden?" I asked. "Who forbade it?"

"The Council of Wise Men in Chelm did."

"Oh, them!" I said. "They're not real. We don't have to listen to them . . . it's not *really* forbidden. Only in a story."

"Have you ever seen a chest with wheels?" asked my grandmother.

"No, never," we said.

"Well, then. It shows that for once, the Council of Wise Men decided something correctly."

"But why did they?" I wanted to know. "Is there a story?"

"Certainly there's a story. The story of Chaim, the poor teacher and his wife, Dvora. Take a pillow each to make the sitting a little softer and I'll tell you."

So Danny and I sat in the chest on two plump pillows and my grandmother told us the story.

"Many years ago, high up on a hill in Chelm, there lived a poor teacher called Chaim and his wife, Dvora. They were so poor that all they had to eat every day was bread with radishes.

Occasionally, an onion came their way. Dvora would take a few onion rings and boil them up with water and salt, throw in a couple of chicken feet that the butcher gave away because no one wanted them, and this mixture she would call 'soup'.

'The rich,' said Chaim, as he drank the colourless liquid from a spoon, 'have fluffy dumplings to go in their soup, made from matzo meal and chicken fat and egg, flavoured with nutmeg and sprinkled with parsley. Their soup is yellow, the colour of gold . . . one soup for the rich and one for the poor . . .' and he would sigh and dip his spoon into the bowl.

'When was the last time,' Dvora asked, 'that we tasted cake?' Chaim thought. 'Six months ago, at the wedding of the rabbi's daughter. Do you remember it?'

Dvora sighed. 'How could I forget it, a cake like that. Filled with chopped nuts and honey and apples, and sprinkled with cinnamon. Such a cake! A cake to dream about.'

Chaim pulled thoughtfully on his beard. 'Wife,' he said at last, 'I have a plan. A plan that will result in our very own cake.'

'Tell me,' said Dvora. 'A cake is what I would dearly like.'

'This is the plan. Do you remember my grandfather's big chest? The one on wheels? Well, we will make a small hole in the lid and lock the chest and give the key to a neighbour to keep. Then, every Friday, just before you light the Sabbath candles, you will put one penny into the chest. And every week before the Sabbath, I will put a penny in also. We are so poor that the loss of two pennies each week will make no difference to our wealth, but the pennies will add up, and in a year, or maybe even nine months, there will be enough in the chest to make the richest, tastiest cake in the whole history of Chelm.'

And so it was agreed. The very next Friday, Chaim put his penny into the chest. Before she lit the Sabbath candles, Dvora went to the chest and dropped her penny into it. Both Chaim and Dvora began to have dreams about the kind of cake it would be . . . Perhaps a plum cake? Or one with shavings of chocolate over the top? Thinking about the cake filled their minds every waking moment and for half the night as well.

By Thursday of the following week however, Chaim had reached a decision. He was a teacher, and therefore a thinker, and his thoughts had been travelling along this path: 'If Dvora puts a penny in the chest every Friday, there will easily be enough pennies after a year to make a perfectly adequate cake. Why should I waste my penny (which Heaven knows I'm desperately in need of) when Dvora's penny will be quite sufficient? No, I will keep my money and say not a word to Dvora and spend it on something else . . . something I need now.' So Chaim went off to the Synagogue that Friday without putting anything into the chest, and continued putting nothing in it, week after week after week.

Meanwhile Dvora (who had the day-to-day cooking to do, don't forget) said to herself: 'I have little enough money to spend as it is. Why should I make myself poorer when Chaim is putting in quite enough money for both of us? After all, what does it matter if the cake is a little smaller, a little less rich? To us, it will still taste like Paradise. No, I will keep my penny and say not a word to Chaim, and try and find a marrow bone for proper soup for once.' So she stopped putting her pennies into the chest. Well, the weeks passed and the months passed and when springtime came, Dvora said: 'It's April, Chaim. Nearly a year since we started collecting money for our cake. Let us go and open the chest and count the pennies and plan our wonderful treat.'

Dvora went to fetch the key from the neighbour and together husband and wife approached the chest. Chaim bent to unlock it. As he opened the lid, Dvora started screaming: 'Oh, Chaim, Chaim we've been robbed! Look! There are only two pennies left . . . oh, who could have done such a wicked thing?' Now Chaim was not clever (because everyone in Chelm is a fool, do you remember?), but he *was* a teacher and therefore could at least put two and two together.

'Don't be silly!' he said to Dvora. 'How could anyone have taken our money? Did you not see me with your own eyes unlock the chest, not half a minute ago? No, I accuse you, wife, of not being honest. I say you have tricked me! You have not been putting in your penny every week, have you?'

Dvora covered her face with her apron and started crying. '*I* have tricked you? Oh, you monster! How can you accuse me when you are the scoundrel? How? *You* have never put a penny in the chest either. And now we've got nothing . . . No pennies and no cake and almost a whole year gone.' She dropped her apron, and began to shake her husband until his teeth rattled. He snarled at her, and the long and the short of it was, they both fell into the chest, and the lid slammed down on top of them and snapped tight shut. Well then, Chaim and Dvora began to push and struggle to get out like two kittens in a pillow-case, and the violent movement set the wheels of the chest rolling, and it rolled right out of the house and down the hill into the main street. As you can imagine, the citizens of Chelm had no idea what was happening. There they were, quietly minding their business when suddenly, along came a huge wooden contraption, careering towards them, ready to crush them to pulp. And not only that, dreadful screams and shrieks were coming from the inside of the chest, so that half the people of Chelm were convinced that all the devils of Hell were bundled up in there, and ran away in one direction, while the other half (composed mainly of children and dogs) chased after the chest, adding their cries to the ones issuing from within its wooden depths. In the end the chest stopped rolling right in front of the Synagogue. The Chief Sage (yes, wearing his golden shoes on his hands!) came out and quickly sent for a locksmith.

When the locksmith opened the chest and Chaim and Dvora popped out, all dishevelled and with their clothes torn and dusty, everyone stepped back in amazement. The Council of Wise Men listened to what the teacher and his wife had to say and the Chief Sage invited them both to his house for the evening, because it just so happened that his wife had baked a cake that day. Two important laws were passed in Chelm shortly after that. The first was that no teacher should ever live at the top of a hill, and the second law was that from that day to this, no chest is allowed to have wheels on it. Now jump out of there, both of you, and help me to push this boat of yours back into the corner."

The Garden of
Talking Flowers

Y grandmother's flat had no garden, but on the balcony at the front of the building she kept a collection of small, reddish-brown flowerpots with spiky cacti growing in them. There were also two bigger earthenware tubs, overflowing with geraniums. Watering the flowerpots was one of the tasks I enjoyed best. My grandmother would fill a jug with water, and I would carry it out of the kitchen and carefully round two sides of the table in the dining-room and out on to the balcony. The earth around each cactus was cracked and dry and almost the same colour as the flowerpots, but as soon as I poured some water on to it from my jug, it became a wonderful, dark shiny brown, like melted chocolate, and all the little cracks would disappear. I enjoyed pouring water so much that sometimes the soil round the plants couldn't soak it up fast enough and it came out of the bottom of the pot and spread over the pale yellow tiles of the balcony floor. These tiles had flower-patterns cut into them, and my grandmother never minded them getting wet, because the sun dried them almost at once. I liked pouring water on the tiles. From being butter-yellow, they turned khaki-colour when they were wet, and I always felt that it was only fair to give some nourishment to the poor thirsty flower-shapes cut into the stone.

A real garden was something we only saw on walks around the city. We'd go down the hill and turn left, and along narrow streets where the houses almost seemed to meet above our heads. We looked into courtyards as we passed, to see what people were growing. In one house, the families had turned the courtyard into a small garden with trees and flowers blooming right in the middle of the building. On our walks we would see avenues of pepper trees, and hedges heavy with pale blue plumbago flowers, and everywhere we could smell the fragrance of pine trees. There was an almond tree outside

Genzel's shop, looking out of place on the grey pavement.

"They built the houses and the streets around it," my grand-mother said "and now everyone looks at it as the winter ends, and waits for the pink and white blossoms to tell them spring is here. The almond tree always blooms for the festival of Tu B'Shvat." She sang me the song:

> The almond tree in flower,
> The bright sun in the sky,
> Birds up on the highest roof
> Sing that Tu B'Shvat is nigh.
>
> Tu B'Shvat is here now,
> Almond blossom time!
> Tu B'Shvat is here now,
> Almond blossom time!

A little way away from my grandmother's flat, across the road and on the corner of the next street, was Moshe's flower shop. Whenever we went visiting, my grandmother would go into this shop and order a bunch of flowers. Moshe or his wife, Mazal, would walk about with us, in and out of the giant vases standing on the floor, while we chose what we wanted: pale pink gladioli, perhaps, so tall that they seemed to me like thin tree branches waving above my head, or red carnations, or the tightly-curled-up buds of yellow roses. I loved to watch Moshe take the flowers and wrap them in whispery sheets of paper and tie a beautiful ribbon around the stems. The shop smelled green and moist. It smelled of earth and moss and fern and hundreds and hundreds of flowers. In summer, Moshe kept the shutters closed to protect the flowers from the sun, and stepping into the shop was like entering a cool, dark cave.

My grandmother took a bunch of flowers with her when she went out for a visit, and many people who came to the flat brought her flowers. She never arranged them while the visitors were still there, but as soon as they'd gone, she would take out the vases and put the flowers in, one by one, and I would help her.

"Which do you like best?" I asked one day. "Carnations or gladioli or roses?"

"Why do I have to like one best?" asked my grandmother. "Can't I like them all? It reminds me of a story."

"What story?"

"A story about a garden. Sit there while I put these flowers in water and I'll tell it to you."

"Was it a big garden? What did it have growing in it?"

"This garden," said my grandmother "was the biggest and most beautiful garden in the whole history of the world. Not since Adam and Eve were banished from Paradise has there been such a garden. In it grew every kind of flower from the daisy to the rose, there were fountains and peacocks and trellises and terraces and arbours and benches and streams and trees of every description: noble cedars, slender cypresses, flowering almonds and orchards and orchards of fruit trees. This was a garden as large as a city. No one knew who owned it, but whoever it was must have been extraordinarily rich and powerful, because not only was this garden magnificent, it was also magical."

"Magical?" I asked. "How was it magical?"

"Because," said my grandmother "every single plant and creature in this garden could talk."

"Wonderful!" I said.

"Well, it was wonderful in one way and in another, it caused a great deal of trouble. The reason it caused trouble was this: as the plants and flowers had nothing better to do, they began to boast, each one saying how beautiful she was, and how much better she was than her neighbour. The air, as well as being filled with the fragrance of the flowers was also, alas, filled with their voices.

'Look at me,' said the poppy. 'My petals are much more delicate than anyone else's and no one can match my scarlet.'

'But your petals tear so easily,' remarked the oleander. 'Just one puff of wind and you're in tatters.'

'That's a typically poisonous remark,' sniffed an orchid that looked very like a small dragon, 'from a poisonous flower. Quite what I'd expect.'

'No need to get agitated,' said the lofty gladiolus in a languid tone. 'I can't imagine anyone being preferred to me. See the economical way that I arrange my flowers all along my stem. And there are so many of them!'

'Some plants,' whispered one carnation to another, 'try to dazzle us with their quantity in the hope that we will not remark upon their quality.'

'Quite so,' answered the second carnation. 'And it would be hard to find a better-quality flower than us: such a range of colours, such fragrance, such frilly petals and so long-lasting. Is it any wonder we are so often chosen for button-holes?'

'I,' said the pale lily, 'would be mortified if I were chosen as a button-hole. I am elegance and purity itself. I have been told so, often and often.'

'No one even notices us,' muttered the daisies, 'making the grass look pretty day after day, getting trodden on all the time with not so much as a word of apology . . . people don't even think of us as proper flowers.'

The rose smiled. 'You may all chatter and quarrel among yourselves. We know, and anyone who knows anything at all knows, that the rose is the queen of any garden. As far as I'm concerned, there's nothing to discuss.'

The trees growing in the garden heard the flowers bickering among themselves.

'Those flowers,' murmured the pine tree. 'I don't know why they give themselves such airs. They grow, they are cut down, they die. We trees, on the other hand, are useful. We provide shelter for birds and animals, we live almost forever. We give fruit year after year, and when we are cut down, the wood from our trunks and branches makes houses where people can live.'

'We should have a contest,' said the willow tree, 'to see which of all the plants in the garden is the very best.'

'But who will judge the contest?' whispered the cedar.

'I will,' said the Dove. 'I will fly through the length and breadth of the garden and look at every flower, tree and shrub, and then I will give my judgement.'

The trees agreed and rustled the message on to the flowers, who became very excited at the thought of a contest. It was to take place on the very next Thursday afternoon. All the flowers preened themselves and made an effort to put out their newest, freshest buds on Thursday morning. The trees arranged their leaves to the best advantage, and urged birds to spring-clean their nests for the occasion. On Thursday morning, the Dove flew for the last time through the garden, noticing the curling petals of the peony, the wax-white flowers on the camellia, and the weight of blossom on the branches of the apricot tree . . . and noticing also one tree that stood apart from the others, its trunk old and twisted, its leaves a dull greyish-green, its roots in rocky soil. The Dove fluttered round this tree and came to rest on one of its branches.

'Trees and flowers of this wonderful garden,' said the Dove. 'Listen to me. I have made my judgement. I have flown round and round this place, looking at everything. It is true that the rose is the most beautiful of the flowers.'

'There, what did I tell you?' said the rose in a loud whisper, her stem bending graciously this way and that, her face elegantly framed by new green leaves.

'But,' the Dove went on 'the rose pricks the fingers of those who try to pluck her, and so in the end, I decided to award the greatest honour to a tree.'

'Which tree? Which tree?' murmured every leaf in the garden.

'Why, this very tree that I am sitting on now,' said the Dove. 'The olive tree.'

None of the other trees could understand it. The olive tree was old and twisted. Its leaves were dull. How could it possibly compare with the dignity of the cedar, the elegance of the cypress, the beauty of the willow?

'I will explain to you all,' said the Dove 'why I have chosen the olive tree. There are four reasons. Firstly, because its fruit, unlike the fruit of the apple, the pear, the plum and the apricot, is salty and sharp and when pressed, yields a nourishing and fragrant oil. Secondly, because the olive does not flaunt its beautiful wood, but hides it under a rough bark. Thirdly, because the olive gives its fruit willingly, even though it is shaken and beaten with sticks, and lastly, because God's own Dove chose an olive branch to take to Noah to show him that the flood was at an end. The olive tree therefore combines usefulness and beauty, modesty and kindness and is a symbol of peace in the world. I could choose no other.'

All the trees were silent after the Dove's judgement. The flowers, too, had to agree that what the Dove said had been most sensible. Only the rose still thought she should have been chosen, but she kept her thoughts to herself and harmony was restored to the garden."

The Market of Miseries

EVERY week, my grandmother spent the whole of Friday preparing for the Sabbath, the day of rest when no cooking could be done and when work of every kind was forbidden. The Sabbath began on Friday at dusk and ended on Saturday, as soon as three stars became visible in the sky.

There were rules in my grandmother's kitchen, and everyone had to follow them.

"It's a Kosher kitchen," she explained to me. "Everything is done according to very ancient laws. I have two sets of everything: knives, forks, plates, pots and pans. One set is for dishes cooked with meat, and the other for dishes with milk in them. Milk and meat must never be mixed." I did not understand exactly why these rules were important, but I was careful, when I dried the knives and forks, to use the towel with the red stripe across it for the meat things, and the one with the blue stripe for milk dishes.

I enjoyed all the preparations. In the kitchen, there was the food to cook, and once that was done, it had to be packed very carefully into a large, square, metal tin that sat on top of a little stove, which burned with a tiny blue flame, all through Friday night and for most of Saturday.

I used to help my grandmother with the food. Because I wasn't allowed near the frying-pan, I sat at the kitchen table and dipped pearly slices of fish, first into beaten egg, then into matzo meal, ready for my grandmother to cook. The pieces of fish made a loud hissing noise as they touched the hot oil, and pale blue smoke rose up and up and disappeared before it reached the ceiling. Another task I was allowed to help with was packing the eggs. I had to shell about a dozen hard-boiled eggs and put them carefully into a dish. This dish had a cover which fitted tightly over the top. When the eggs went in on Friday, they were white with clear yellow yolks, just as you would expect, but as if by magic, when we took them out on Saturday, the whites were the colour of coffee with cream in it, and the yolks had turned into small moons: pale, pale yellow edged with a bluish grey.

"It's from standing all night long and cooking," my grand-mother explained, but I still believed it was magic. Nothing else that cooked all night changed colour. The largest pot of all contained the cholent: a stew made with beans and potatoes and meat that was so tender when you ate it that it fell into soft strands in your mouth and sometimes became stuck between your teeth. Then there were flasks of tea and coffee, and airtight tins full of strudel and cinnamon biscuits, and of course, the kugel.

There was another kitchen task I liked, although I never did it on a Friday, and that was cleaning the rice. My grandmother would shake the rice out of a big, brown paper bag on to a round brass tray, and spread it out for me, so that it covered all the curly patterns of leaves and flowers scratched on to the metal. The rice made a thin hard sound as it fell on to the tray, like the sound of hailstones bouncing off a window. I had to push the grains around with my fingers and find the horrible, blackened ones, and remove them to a little plate my grand-mother put next to the tray.

It was fortunate that the Sabbath was a day for visits, because otherwise I would have been very bored indeed. No sewing nor writing was allowed, and I was too young to be able to read. What I did was listen. My grandmother's friends would sit and drink tea and eat biscuits and strudel, and talk and talk. Their talk, if I understood it at all, seemed to me to be mainly complaints: about their husbands, children, about shopkeepers, about life in general. I said so to my grandmother.

"Everyone enjoys a good 'kvetch' now and then," she said.

"What's a kvetch?" I wanted to know.

"A complaint. A moan. A kvetch is also the name for someone who whines. 'She's a real kvetch' you say. I'll tell you a story about a kvetch. Listen. Once upon a time, long ago, there lived a woman called Zilpa. She was married and had two children, a son and a daughter. She had a sister, and a mother-in-law. She had two friends called Mina and Rina. And all she did, all day long, from morning till night, was complain.

'My husband never listens to me,' she would say. 'He sits all day long with his head in a book and if I speak to him he either nods or grunts or both. Oh, how I wish I could have a more attentive husband. Can there be a more annoying characteristic in a man?'

Then she would complain about her son. 'Lazy? I never saw anything like it in my life. Why, if he could manage to go to school lying down, then he would. Why do other mothers have such diligent, hard-working sons, when I am saddled with a slug-a-bed?'

When she had finished on the subject of her son, Zilpa would go on to her daughter. 'God has given me an untidy daughter. She will never marry, and if she does, her husband will divorce her in a week, she is so messy. Why, the other day I went into her room and it took me half an hour to find the door again, such a dreadful upheaval there was in there.'

On the subject of her mother-in-law, she was at her loudest. 'Nothing I do for her son is good enough! Why is it I who have to suffer such a pernickety creature for a mother-in-law? Why is it not my sister? Oh, no, she has all the luck. Her mother-in-law hardly dares to open her mouth, let alone criticize. And while I think of my sister, why does she live in such a fine house on the fashionable side of town, while I survive in this hovel with my inattentive husband, lazy son, messy daughter and carping mother-in-law?'

You are probably wondering who Zilpa was complaining to, when she spoke in this way about the various members of her family. The answer is: to her friends, Mina and Rina. What else are friends for, if not to listen to a person's innermost kvetches? But naturally (once a kvetch, always a kvetch!) moaning to Mina and Rina did not prevent Zilpa from telling her family a few home truths about her friends.

'That Mina,' she would say to her mother-in-law, 'she never invites us to her house . . . never. Sits and drinks gallons of tea in my house, and her own weight in sugared almonds, but will she invite us to her house? When the Messiah comes, maybe. And Rina never stops talking, not even to draw breath . . . my this . . . my that . . . never a word about anyone else's concerns. And you wouldn't believe some of the things she says about people! It wouldn't surprise me at all if she spreads wicked lies about me. It's no more than I would expect.'

And so, Zilpa's life went on – one long, unending, never-changing kvetch. The noise of her complaints grew and grew, until at last it reached the ears of the Angels in Heaven.

'Go to that woman,' said the Chief Angel to one of the Lesser Angels, 'and direct her to the Market of Miseries.' So the Lesser Angel took on the shape of a pedlar, and called on Zilpa one morning.

'I don't know what you think you're going to sell me,' said Zilpa. 'I haven't a penny to spare. Nothing ever goes right for me. Other women manage to have enough money to buy a length of ribbon if it takes their fancy, but not me, oh no. I'm sorry. You've come to the wrong house.'

'I can see,' said the Angel, who was as clever as all angels are, 'that you are an extremely unfortunate lady. Someone as intelligent and charming as you are shouldn't have to be worried about money.'

Zilpa thought: what a delightful man! How rare to come across someone so understanding! She said, 'It's not only the money, you know. There's my inattentive husband, my lazy son, my messy daughter, my pernickety mother-in-law and my unsatisfactory friends.'

'Tsk! Tsk!' said the Angel-pedlar. 'It seems to me that you should pay a visit to the Market of Miseries.'

'The Market of Miseries?' said Zilpa. 'I've never heard of it.'

'I would have to take you there,' smiled the pedlar. 'It is, of course, not open to everyone. Only to very special, worthy people.'

'Goodness!' said Zilpa. 'It sounds very interesting. Will it take long? To get there, I mean, and to come back?'

'Not long at all,' said the pedlar. 'It is twelve o'clock now. We will be back before you can blink.' That, Zilpa thought, was probably an exaggeration. She took off her apron, picked up her basket and called out to her husband, who was in the house:

'I'm going to the market! Back in an hour . . .'

'Mmmm,' said her husband from deep in the house.

'Do you see what I mean?' Zilpa asked the pedlar.

'Indeed. Follow me,' said the pedlar, and began to walk away from Zilpa's front door. She walked behind him. The streets of the city, the streets she recognized, soon gave way to a rough track which wound between fields studded with boulders. The Angel-pedlar and Zilpa walked and walked.

This market, Zilpa was thinking, is very far away. I will never be back before one o'clock. And there's nobody here . . . not anywhere. Who has ever heard of a market with no people? I should never have followed this man . . . perhaps he will kill me and leave my body by the side of the road . . . And Zilpa began to tremble.

'Here we are,' said the pedlar, and pointed into the distance. Yes, Zilpa thought, I can see something . . . perhaps the outskirts of another town . . . yes, yes, there are awnings flapping . . . people . . . market stalls . . . oh, how marvellous!

The pedlar turned to her. 'You have complained about your husband, your children, your sister, your mother-in-law and your friends. Therefore, you may walk about wherever you wish in this market, and choose other faults for all of them . . . and then they will cease to be as they are, and will be as you wish them to be.'

'Thank you,' said Zilpa, and began to walk about among the stalls.

'Husband?' said the first stall-holder, who was dressed in red from head to toe, with a red veil hiding her face, 'I can offer you cruelty, drunkenness, ignorance, meanness, a love of gambling, infidelity, violence, lack of humour, or inattentiveness.'

'Oh, my word!' said Zilpa. 'I've never thought about it before . . . I suppose, out of all those, inattentiveness is the best.'

'I'll wrap it up for you,' said the veiled stall-holder, and she put a small parcel into Zilpa's basket.

The next stall-holder was dressed in blue, and veiled like her neighbour. 'Children's faults!' she called out. 'Come and choose! Lovely wide variety! Dishonesty, stupidity, dislike of parents, a longing to leave home, rages, sulking, laziness, messiness . . . all bargains . . . come and choose.'

'I suppose,' said Zilpa 'laziness and messiness, please.' Two more small parcels found their way into Zilpa's basket.

'Sisters?' said the next stall-holder, dressed from head to toe in yellow, with yellow veils over her face. 'You can have them envious, spiteful, flirtatious, two-faced, unkind, luckier than you are . . .'

Zilpa sighed. 'What can I say? Luckier than me, I suppose.'

'Here you are, then' said the yellow-draped figure, and another parcel was added to those in Zilpa's basket. The stall-holder on the mother-in-law stall was wearing green. 'Can I tempt you?' she said. 'Jealousy, ill-health, drunkenness, idleness, extravagance, lying, a sharp tongue, fussiness. The choice is yours.'

'Fussiness, please,' said Zilpa. Her basket was nearly full now. Only the stall for friends was left for her to visit.

'Friends!' the stall-holder said, from behind her purple veil, 'spitefulness, envy, betrayal, meanness, gossiping, ill-wishing, tale-bearing, visiting too often and not inviting you back . . .'

'I'll have visiting too often, and gossiping,' said Zilpa.

The Angel-pedlar appeared suddenly at Zilpa's side.

'Are you ready?' he said. 'There is only one more stall to visit. It's the place where you may pick a Supplementary Misery, if you wish. Or not, if you choose not to.'

'What are they, these supplementary miseries?'

'All sorts of things . . . assorted ailments from pimples to the plague, hunger, pain, poverty, war, anguish . . . on a good day, one can even find Death.'

'No, no,' said Zilpa. 'Thank you very much. I'm very satisfied with what I've got. I won't be needing any supplementary miseries.'

'Very well,' said the pedlar. 'Then I shall take you home.'

Before Zilpa could say another word, there she was, back in her own courtyard. The pedlar was nowhere to be seen. She glanced down at her basket, and was astonished to see, instead of the miseries she had collected in the market, seven ripe pomegranates. She went into the house and looked at the clock.

'It must have stopped,' she said to herself. 'It still says twelve o'clock.' But the clock was ticking loudly.

'I've just been to the market,' said Zilpa to her husband, who looked up and smiled.

'You told me that just a moment ago,' he said. 'I expect you thought I wasn't listening, as usual. You also told me it took an hour.'

Zilpa was just about to correct her husband, when she stopped herself. Better to say nothing, she thought. I must have been dreaming. She went into the kitchen to put the pomegranates away, and the pedlar returned to the Gates of

Heaven, where he was welcomed by all the other angels.

'It never fails,' said the Chief Angel. 'Never. When people have a chance of choosing their misfortunes, out of all the available shapes and sizes of miseries offered to them, they always, always choose the ones they already know: their own.'

And all the angels laughed heartily at human beings, and at how predictable they were."

An Overcrowded House

I N the entrance hall of my grandmother's flat, there was a cupboard set so high up in the wall that only a tall person standing on a chair could open it. Luckily, my grandmother needed what was kept up there once a year only, so it had to be reached on two occasions: once, to bring out the Passover dishes ready for the Festival, every spring, and the second time to put them all away for another twelve months. My tallest cousin, Arieh, was always the person who had to stand on the chair and pass down dishes and cups and plates, knives and forks and pots and pans and glasses to my grandmother and me, waiting to carry them to the kitchen.

At Passover time, all the ordinary dishes were put away and the whole flat was cleaned from top to bottom. Not a single crumb was allowed to lurk forgotten in the corner. Holes in the wall had to be plastered over. Sometimes, my grandmother decided that this or that room needed whitewashing, and she would pile all the furniture into the middle of the room for a day, and cover it with sheets, and then slap a thick, white sloppy brush up and down the walls.

"Why do you have the best things hidden away in the cupboard all the time?" I asked my grandmother. "Why are they only allowed down into the house for a week?"

"Because it's a special celebration," said my grandmother. "It's to celebrate the escape of the Jews from their captivity in Egypt. We will read the whole story again, on the night of the First Seder."

For the Seder the door between the dining-room and the room where the long, blue sofa was, was folded back, and the table was pulled out to its full length. More than twenty people would sit around it for the Passover meal, eating matzos and bitter herbs and drinking sweet wine, and telling the story of the Plagues that God sent down to the land of Egypt. In the Hagadah, the book we looked at as the meal continued, there were coloured drawings of the Plagues: frogs, locusts, boils, and a very frightening picture showing a dead child covered in blood, and representing the Death of the First Born. There was also a picture of Moses parting the Red Sea, with high, blue waves towering above the heads of the Israelites like walls of sapphire. We sang songs, and waited up till late at night to see whether this year, the prophet Elijah would come and drink the glass of wine my grandmother always put out for him. At the end of the meal, my cousins and I would run all over the flat searching for the Afikoman. This was half a matzo, wrapped in a napkin, which my grandmother hid like a treasure. Whoever found it won a small prize: an apple or a square of chocolate. There were so many cousins rushing about that I never managed to find the Afikoman, but my grandmother gave us all apples and chocolate too, so I didn't mind.

"It's not very fair for the winner, though," I said to my grandmother. "It makes winning less special."

"Nonsense," said my grandmother. "Finding the Afikoman is an honour and it brings good luck. And looking all over the place is fun, too."

In spite of the special dishes, and the book with pictures of the Plagues, in spite of the sips of sweet wine and the brown-freckled matzos which tasted so delicious with strawberry jam on them, I was always quite glad when the festival was over and the visitors went home. Then I could have my grandmother to myself again and she could tell me stories.

"You don't know," she said "How well off you are. I should tell you the story of Mordechai and Chaya. Once upon a time, there was a farmer called Mordechai, who lived in a miserable little farmhouse right on the edge of the village. He had two muddy fields next to the house, where he tried to grow this and that and the other. I have to tell you that most of the time he failed miserably, and when Chaya took the farm produce to the market and set it out on a stall, people walked by with their noses in the air saying: 'Pshaw! Such cabbages I wouldn't feed to my chickens! Do you call this a turnip? This is a turnip's wizened grandfather! And this is not a potato, this is a joke . . .' and so forth. But Chaya didn't laugh. The money grew scarcer and scarcer, and the couple grew more and more miserable. Then, one terrible day, Mordechai's father died, leaving Mordechai's mother penniless. She had to sell her house to pay her late husband's debts, and so there she was, homeless at her age. Well, there was no alternative: the poor old lady had to move in at once with Mordechai and Chaya. It was difficult to know quite where to put her. The farmhouse was really two rooms: one large room, with a corner curtained off to hide the bed where Mordechai and Chaya slept, and one tiny room which the couple called the kitchen, but which could more accurately have been called a cupboard with a window. When Mordechai's mother moved in, he hung a curtain across another corner of the large room, to hide the bed she had brought with her, and tried to make the best of it. But it was difficult.

'What shall we do?' he asked Chaya. 'She snores at night and keeps me awake.'

'She squeezes into the kitchen to help me cook,' said Chaya, 'so that I can hardly move. I think you should go and see the Rabbi. Ask his advice.'

'What good will that do?' asked Mordechai.

'What harm will it do?' his wife replied.

So in the end, Mordechai went to the Rabbi and told him all his troubles. This rabbi was not as clever as Rabbi Samuels, but he wasn't a fool. He listened to Mordechai, and muttered and mumbled into his beard, and fixed his eyes on an interesting spot on the ceiling, and finally he turned to Mordechai.

'Have you any livestock?' he asked.

'A few chickens . . . a goat . . . a cow to give milk . . . nothing much, I assure you.'

'Take the chickens,' said the Rabbi 'and move them into the house with you.'

'Into the house?' Mordechai thought the Rabbi had gone mad.

'Exactly,' said the Rabbi, 'do as I say and your troubles will soon be over.'

Mordechai did as the Rabbi said. Never had he and Chaya been so miserable. The chickens squawked all day and got under everyone's feet. They laid eggs in unexpected places and flew on to the table at mealtimes to share what little food there was. The rooster had decided that Mordechai and Chaya's brass bedstead was his perch, and there, every morning he would split the dawn in half with his crowing. Mordechai and Chaya used to leap out of their skins in fright.

'Go back to the Rabbi,' said Chaya. 'Tell him everything is ten times worse than before.'

So Mordechai went and poured out all his woes to the Rabbi. The Rabbi muttered and mumbled into his beard and fixed his eyes on an interesting spot on the back of the door, and then finally he turned to Mordechai.

'You said you had a cow?' he asked.

'Yes . . . one cow.'

'Bring the cow into the house,' said the Rabbi.

'Where will I put her?'

'Tie her up to the handle of the door,' said the Rabbi. 'All your troubles will soon be over.'

Mordechai returned to the farmhouse and told his wife what the Rabbi had said.

'He has taken leave of his senses,' said Chaya. 'But he is an educated man, so we should at least try it.'

Life immediately went from bad to worse. No one could move in or out of the door without bumping into the cow. Twice, she pulled the rickety door off its hinges, and once chewed up both the curtain hiding Mordechai's mother's bed and some of her blankets as well.

'Go back to the Rabbi,' said Chaya after a week had passed. 'Tell him everything is a hundred times worse than before.'

So Mordechai went and cried out his anguish to the Rabbi. The Rabbi muttered and mumbled into his beard and fixed his eyes on an interesting spot on the floor and then finally he turned to Mordechai.

'Do you still have a goat?'

'Yes . . . one goat.'

'Bring the goat into the house.'

'Where will I put him?'

'Tie him up to the end of your bed,' said the Rabbi 'and your troubles will soon be over.'

Mordechai returned to the farmhouse. When he told Chaya what the Rabbi had said, she couldn't believe her ears.

'The Rabbi is bewitched,' she cried. 'What is he telling us to do? Look at my house. Look what he has made us do already . . .

there are chickens wherever you look, clucking and squawking and dropping eggs and feathers all over the floor, the cow knocks over all the furniture and pulls the door off its hinges, my linen drawer has become a manger full of straw, and now he wants us to bring in the goat as well . . . and tie him to the end of our bed. It's too much!' She sat down at the table and wept salty tears into the dough she had been kneading.

'But you said yourself,' said Mordechai 'he is an educated man, and so we should at least try it.' So Chaya wiped her tears away and went to fetch the goat.

The next day, Chaya went with Mordechai to see the Rabbi. They sat at the table and Chaya spoke first.

'My husband has been to you before,' she said 'and you have advised him and we have followed your advice. Yesterday you told us to bring in the goat, and we did it, and today we are both three-quarters of the way to our graves. It wasn't the fact that the goat ate every single thing it could reach, including a piece from my husband's nightshirt. After all, what do I own that's too precious for a goat to eat? Nothing, that's what. No, Rabbi, what finally drove us to seek your help is the stench. Have you ever slept within three feet of a goat? I thought my last hour had come. We have not slept a wink all night. Tell us, Rabbi, what do we do now?'

The Rabbi did not mutter, nor did he mumble. He did not fix his eyes on interesting spots anywhere in the room. Instead, he spoke straight to Mordechai and Chaya.

'Take the goat and the cow and the chickens out of your house. Return them to their own quarters. Then clean your house from top to bottom, and come and tell me how you feel.'

Two days later, Mordechai and Chaya returned to the Rabbi's house.

'Oh, thank you, thank you, Rabbi,' they said. 'Our house is restored to us. It is clean and quiet and it doesn't smell of goat!'

'But what about Mordechai's mother? Do you not find it crowded?' said the Rabbi.

'Crowded?' said Mordechai. 'It's like a palace.'

'Paradise!' agreed Chaya. 'I shall never complain about it ever again.'

And she never did."

A Phantom at the Wedding

ALL sorts of people came to visit my grandmother. The most frequent visitors were members of the family: her sons and daughters and her grandchildren, her brother, his children and their children, and representatives of other, more distant branches of the family tree.

Then there were my grandmother's friends. I liked it when these ladies came to call because they generally wore necklaces and brooches that twinkled and glittered against the navy blue,

or olive green, or brown or black of their dresses. They would kiss me and feel my hair and hug me close to their bosoms till I could smell the sugary fragrance of their face powder. If I admired their jewels, they would take them off at once, and pin them on me or drape them round my neck, and I would run off to the shoe cupboard and put on a pair of my aunt Sara's shoes, just to complete the magnificence of my outfit. These ladies drank tea and ate cake and talked to my grandmother about their children and their grandchildren and listened to her stories, but sometimes there was another kind of visitor to the flat.

The bell would ring and I would go and open the door – only to find a ragged old man with a wispy white beard standing there, looking at me from under the brim of a black felt hat. My grandmother had several men like this who came ringing at the door, and they were all old and all had wispy grey beards and wore black hats and long black coats that nearly touched the floor. They would shuffle into the dining-room and sit muttering to my grandmother in Yiddish for a while, and then they would go shuffling away again. They never ate or drank anything while they were in the flat. I asked my grandmother once who they were.

"They are Jews who do not have enough money. All they do all day is study the word of God, and then sometimes they come and collect money from richer people, people like us."

"Don't they earn money, for reading about God all day?"

"Not very much, I'm afraid. So they collect from various houses, and giving them charity is a duty and a blessing."

"Have you got enough money to give some to all of them?" I

wanted to know. "Will there be enough left for us?" My grandmother laughed. "Of course! And in any case, no one should have too much money. It's bad for you, like too much food."

"Bad for you?" I was amazed. "How can it be bad for you. If you had a lot of money, you could have anything you liked."

"But too much money makes you extremely selfish. Look, I'll show you, just in the way that one of the ancient Rabbis showed a miser about selfishness, long ago. Go and look out of the window."

I went and looked down into the street.

"What can you see?" asked my grandmother.

"The street . . . cars . . . the Eiges's flat. Someone is beating a carpet . . . Moshe and Mazal's shop . . . Genzel's . . ."

"What else?"

"People walking about."

"Exactly," said my grandmother. "How many people?"

"A lot . . . two men. A woman and a dog. A group of children . . . some big, some little . . . All kinds of people."

"Now touch the window." I touched it. "What is it made of?" she continued.

"It's made of glass," I said.

"Quite right. Now come with me to the bedroom." I followed her down the corridor and stood in front of the mirrored panel of the big, brown cupboard.

"What can you see now?" asked my grandmother.

"I can see myself."

"Just you?"

"Just me."

"Now touch the mirror," said my grandmother. "What is it made of?"

"I think it's made of glass," I said.

"You're right. It *is* made of glass, exactly like the glass in the window, which you touched a moment ago. But what do you suppose has happened to this glass? Why can't you see anything except yourself?"

I shook my head. "Why?" I asked. "I don't know."

"Because," said my grandmother, "the back of the glass is coated with silver . . . the same silver that money is made from. The ancient Rabbi told the miser that it was silver and nothing but silver which made him see only himself, and which prevented him from seeing other people, and therefore, stopped him from thinking about their welfare."

"Thank you for the story," I said, "but why do those old men never have a cup of tea or a biscuit while they're here?"

"Oh, they're much too devout," said my grandmother. "Even though I keep a strict division in my kitchen between meat dishes and milk dishes, they don't know me well enough to be sure of that, you see, and rather than risk eating something unclean by mistake, they eat and drink nothing at all."

I looked at the closed doors of the big, brown cupboard, then at my grandmother.

"Please may I take out the shawls?" I asked. This was a very special treat. My grandmother kept her shawls on the top shelf. They were beautifully knitted in pale colours and soft wool; lacy, filmy triangles and squares that she wrapped around her shoulders as she sat on the balcony on cool evenings.

"But be careful with them," she said as she brought them down for me. "Don't get the wool caught on anything. What are you going to be today? A princess?"

"A bride," I answered, choosing a huge, white shawl and covering my head with it.

"Can you breathe under there?" asked my grandmother.

"The lace is full of holes," I said. "I can see the whole room with a pattern of white leaves and flowers over it."

"Tell me when the wedding is over," said my grandmother "and I will tell you a story about a bride."

"Tell it to me now," I said "and I'll play later."

My grandmother sighed. "Very well, but at least take the shawl off your face while you listen."

So I took the shawl from over my head and put it round my shoulders as I listened to my grandmother.

"This," she said, "is a story about a ghost. Do you like stories like that?"

"Is it very frightening?"

"No, not very frightening. Perhaps touching would be a better word. Do you remember my Aunt Nehama?"

I nodded. I remembered her well. Aunt Nehama was the oldest person I had ever seen. Her face was lined and creased all over, like a walnut, and her hands were brown and stiff and covered in lumps and bumps: they looked like the twisted roots of a tree. Aunt Nehama never moved. She sat in her house in a high-backed chair at the kitchen table, drinking black coffee and smoking dark yellow cigarettes. She had a black scarf tied round her head. I had been quite glad to come home after visiting her.

My grandmother had told me that it was because she had no teeth left, but still, I didn't like the way her lips seemed to disappear into her mouth in a network of tiny wrinkles.

"You may find this hard to imagine," my grandmother said, "but Nehama was the most beautiful young girl in the whole city. Her skin was like cream, her hair like the finest silk, reaching almost to her waist. Matchmakers came from far and wide to try and arrange a marriage between Nehama and this or that or the other eligible young man. But this story is not about Nehama, but about her grandmother. She told it to Nehama's mother, Nehama's mother told it to her, she told it to me, and now I'm telling it to you. So listen.

Nehama's grandmother was called Ruth. Ruth was a beautiful young woman, but not only beautiful. She was kind-hearted and clever as well. A marriage had been arranged between her and a young man called Asher. On the day that they were introduced, they fell madly in love, and so, as you can imagine, everything was perfect. It was autumn. Ruth and her mother planned to spend the winter sewing and embroidering sheets, pillow-cases, towels, tablecloths and aprons, not to mention preparing drawers full of camisoles and dainty petti-coats and delicate blouses. Then in the spring, for the wedding Ruth would be dressed in a white lace dress with a veil over her face, ready to stand with her beloved Asher under the red velvet canopy which represented the groom's home, and into which he would welcome his bride.

Well, all that sewing and preparation could not possibly be done by Ruth and her mother working by themselves, so all the ladies of the family helped. Ruth's friends came to lend their hands to the task as well, and winter evening after winter evening passed in this way; with skilful hands moving like butterflies over the fabric in the yellow light of lamps. In the corners of the room, over the shoulders of the women sewing, the shadows trembled and shook and stretched. Voices grew quiet and it was quite natural at such a time that minds turned to such things as the spirits of the dead. One particular story was told which saddened Ruth greatly, because she could put herself in the place of the bride in the story, and imagine . . . well, let me tell you the tale as her friends told it to Ruth.

Once, they said, there was a bride who died on the very day of her wedding. In fact she died as she was waiting to walk with her mother and the groom's mother to the bridal canopy. The groom came before the ceremony to look under her veil. This is a tradition that makes quite sure the bride is the one the man has agreed to marry. When this poor groom lifted the veil, there was his future wife pale and waxen as a lily, with all the life gone from her. The rejoicing for the wedding gave way to seven days of black mourning. Tears flowed like wine. But time passed, and gradually the young man grew more interested in life than in remembering his dead bride, and at last, another marriage was arranged for him. But the ghost of the first bride was still wandering the face of the earth, weeping her love. The long and the short of it was: the new bride called off the wedding twenty-four hours before the ceremony, claiming to have seen a spectre dressed in bridal clothes standing at the foot of her bed.

'You should be careful, Ruth,' said all Ruth's friends. 'People say the ghost still visits weddings to this day. What would you do if you saw her? Would you faint?' Ruth answered not a word, but smiled over her stitching.

The days passed and the nights too, and soon the spring came, and it was time for Ruth and Asher to be married. The night before her wedding, when Ruth went into her bedroom to spend her last night under her father's roof, she saw the thin figure of a young girl dressed in white, sitting on the end of her bed and weeping. Ruth knew at once that this was the ghost her friends had spoken of, but so heart-rending was the sound of the ghost's tears, that Ruth was moved to pity.

'What's the matter?' she whispered, 'why are you crying?'

'I am crying,' said the ghost 'because there is to be a wedding and it is not my wedding.'

'But you wouldn't want it to be your wedding,' said Ruth, 'because the person I am marrying is not your love, but mine.'

The ghost turned a stricken face to Ruth. 'But I never stood under the canopy and saw it all twined round with flowers. I never heard the Seven Blessings. No one put a ring on my finger, and I have never heard the glass being crushed beneath my husband's foot. If only I could be part of the ceremony, I could rest easy in my grave forever.'

Ruth took a deep breath. 'Stay here,' she said 'and I will speak to my mother.' She left the room. After an hour, she returned. The ghost was still sitting at the foot of the bed.

'I have spoken to my mother,' said Ruth. 'You may take her place tomorrow. Do you promise to go back to where you came from if I let you stand at my side throughout the ceremony?' The ghost nodded and vanished into thin air.

The next day, Ruth's mother and her friends helped her dress and prepare for the wedding. Lighted candles stood on the table, together with small cut-glass bowls of sugared almonds and raisins for the bride's attendants. Ruth, of course, was not allowed to eat anything until after the wedding.

When Asher came to raise the veil, he found the most beautiful bride in the whole world waiting for him, dressed in white lace like foam, her eyes shining like diamonds.

The guests started to whisper to themselves as the bridal procession made its way to the canopy. The marriage contract had been read, and all was ready for the ceremony.

'But where is the bride's mother?' people said. 'Who is that standing at Ruth's left hand?'

The Rabbi sang the Seven Blessings, the wine was drunk, and at last the glass, wrapped in a white cloth, was crushed under the groom's heel, to symbolize the destruction of the Temple in Jerusalem, and to remind everyone that even in the midst of joy, there were people suffering, somewhere in the world. And through everything, the ghost stood beside the bride, under a velvet canopy at last.

Later, as the music rose into the night sky, and everyone was dancing and making merry, the ghost tapped Ruth on the shoulder.

'Thank you,' she said. 'I will now rest easy in my grave, but I may return to dance at a wedding now and then, to remind myself of past happiness.'

She vanished then, and no one can be sure if she has ever

returned. There is always someone, at every wedding party, someone at the edge of the dancing throng who may or may not be the ghost bride. No one asks any questions . . . they pour the guest another glass of wine, and move on, just in case . . .

Ruth told Nehama's mother the story, and she told Nehama. I cannot vouch for the truth of it, of course, but I was at Nehama's wedding, and spoke for some minutes to a pale young woman whose name I didn't catch and whom I've never seen before or since . . ."

My grandmother got up and went into the kitchen. I put the white shawl over my face like a veil, and looked through the tracery of flowers and leaves at my image in the glass, pretending to be the ghost-bride in my aunt Sara's high-heeled silver sandals.

Later on, my grandmother came to put the shawls away, and helped me to get ready for bed. First, I put on my nightdress, then she brought me a drink of warm milk with honey stirred into it. She waited while I brushed my teeth, and then sat on my bed for a few moments. During the winter months, I always had a fluffy dark blue blanket on my bed. It was exactly the colour of the night sky, and was bound round the edges with a wide blue satin ribbon that I stroked as I fell asleep.

My grandmother left the light on in the corridor. I watched her shadow disappearing and listened to the comforting sound of her voice, rising and falling in the room next to mine.

Golden
Windows

and other stories of Jerusalem

FROM A SHOP IN JERUSALEM

My sister has turned her back to the door.
Avoid it, she says. The street is full of History.
She has made a barricade in the window,
riveted lace with brooch-pins,
heaped underwear against the glass.

My sister says: I am remembering the snow,
up to my knees, billowing like a quilt,
a freight of white on our roof.
My sister tells white stories
in the melting night.
She sings of wolves and forests
in a land of sand and jackals,
where the sun is a flat iron,
pressing and pressing.

Somewhere, we have lacquer boxes
and sandalwood chests.
My sister says: smell the trees.
Look at the painted dolls, filled with smaller dolls.
Our children would have come out dark with blood.

Every so often, the fighting starts again.
My sister says: we live in a place
where armies drive about outside the window.
Avoid wars, she says. Stay away from the door.

Shawls have come from Japan:
flowers opening in silk gardens.
My sister says: hang them in the corner.
Put the roses facing the street.

Adèle Geras

GOLDEN WINDOWS 1910

Harry and his family often came from New York to Jerusalem during the summer holidays to visit his father's family. There were, it seemed to Harry, hundreds of these relatives, but Harry's favourite was his Aunt Rachel.

'You're not really my aunt,' he used to say to her, 'but my great-aunt. It's my dad who's your nephew, not me.'

'An expert on the family tree!' Aunt Rachel would say. 'You're quite right, of course. Leah, my mother, and Miriam, your grandmother, were sisters.'

One of the best things about visiting Aunt Rachel was looking at the photographs. Harry had never seen so many in one place before. Aunt Rachel had a drawer in the bottom of her cupboard that was full of big, brown envelopes, and each envelope was crammed with pictures: small black and white snapshots, sepia studio portraits from long ago, coloured photographs in which he recognised himself and his sisters, and Israeli cousins of his own generation.

'Why don't you put them all into albums, Aunt Rachel? All our photos back home in New York are in albums. It makes them easier to look at.'

'But not so much of an adventure,' said Aunt Rachel, tipping the contents of one brown envelope over the carpet, so that they made a pattern of their own on a rich background of scarlet, black and gold. 'This way you never know who you will find. Look at this, for example.'

She had picked out one of the brown photographs. Harry sighed. He preferred the more recent ones where at least there was a chance that he would see a face he recognised. He looked at the children in the old-fashioned clothes. They were grouped neatly on a sofa which had a huge vase next to it. There were three boys in high collars and uncomfortable-looking jackets, and four girls in frilly, lacy dresses with bows in their hair. The littlest was just a toddler. Aunt Rachel pointed at her.

'That's your grandmother,' she said and Harry laughed. His grandmother had been tall, and elegant with grey hair in a bun and very shiny black shoes. He stared at the chubby smiling baby, and tried to imagine how such a strange transformation could possibly have happened.

'Which sister is that?' he asked, pointing to a small girl who was obviously trying not to burst out laughing. 'I like her.'

'That's Pnina,' said Aunt Rachel, 'who was always having adventures. There are so many stories about Pnina, I hardly know where to start.'

Harry settled himself more comfortably on the sofa. He knew that a story was coming from the dreamy way Aunt Rachel was staring at the photograph in her hand. All he had to do was wait.

*　　　　*　　　　*

The Genzel family lived in four rooms on the first floor of a huge, stone house arranged around the sides of a paved courtyard, in one of the Jewish quarters of Jerusalem: the one called The Hundred Gates. Eight households shared the building, but Zehava Genzel had more children than anyone else: Moshe, Reuben, Eli, Sarah, Leah, Pnina and little Miriam. Pnina was eight years old.

'Poor Mrs Genzel,' the neighbours used to say. 'So young and already a widow.'

'But imagine if her husband had lived on!' whispered others. 'There would be ten children in those rooms by now, and who knows how many more to come? Mr Genzel, blessed be his memory, may have been taken up to Heaven for a very good reason.'

Pnina never thought of her family as especially large, nor did she mind the rooms where they all lived together being so crowded. She even quite enjoyed sharing a bed with Leah, especially during the winter. Leah was six, and slept so quietly that sometimes it looked as though she hadn't moved at all during the night. Once, Pnina decided to watch her through the dark hours, to see if she moved around in bed. For what seemed like a very long time, she stared at her sister lying motionless as a statue, but gradually her eyelids grew heavier and heavier and she fell asleep. In the morning, Leah's position in bed hadn't changed a bit.

Miriam, the youngest child, still slept in her cot next to her sisters' bed, and she used to snuffle and snort in her sleep like a little woodland creature burrowing among fallen leaves. The three boys shared the other bedroom, and Zehava and Sarah, the eldest daughter, slept on beds in the living-room, which were covered up in the morning with rugs and cushions and turned into sofas for the rest of the day, until bedtime.

With so many in the family, Zehava Genzel made sure that every child helped her a little. Pnina, because she was the wanderer and loved to go walking in the streets and looking at everything, was the one chosen to fetch the bread from Greenberg's bakery. Usually, she took Leah with her, or even Miriam, because, as Zehava often said: 'There's safety in numbers.' Pnina couldn't see how Leah or Miriam would help her if she were in any great danger, and suspected that her mother was simply glad of the peace and quiet when the little children were out of the house.

One day in early December, though, Pnina went to fetch the bread by herself. Leah had a cough, and Miriam had fallen asleep on some cushions in a corner of the living-room.

'It's a shame to wake her,' Zehava whispered.

'I'll go on my own,' Pnina whispered back, her heart making loud thumping noises in her ears, for fear that her mother might not let her go. 'I'll be very careful.'

Zehava sighed. 'Very well. I suppose not much

harm can come to you between here and Greenberg's.'

Pnina smiled. 'So can I look in the windows as I pass, to see if I can find a present for Miriam's birthday?'

'I suppose so, but only on the main street. Don't turn off into any of the little alleyways.'

'No,' said Pnina. 'I really won't.'

She set out immediately. It had rained earlier in the day, but now a pale, chilly, wintery sort of sun hung in the blue sky. The paving-stones were still wet, and the smell of damp pine-needles filled the air. Pnina made her way down the hill, out of the district known as The Hundred Gates and into the part of the city that was full of shops selling silver and beaten copper and brass and carpets that vibrated with dark and glowing colours in spell-binding patterns. The streets were crowded with people and carriages drawn by mules, and beggars, and men selling delicious-smelling things to eat which her mother would never buy.

'You don't know how it's been cooked,' she used to say. 'It may be dirty and give you a terrible stomach-ache.' Sometimes Pnina thought it would be worth having a stomach-ache, just to try a mouthful, but maybe not. Maybe a stomach-ache would never stop and she would be ill forever.

Pnina decided to buy the bread first and look for a present for Miriam on the way home. Mrs Greenberg put the three plaited loaves into the string bag for her, and said:

'Such a big girl you're getting! Fetching the bread

all by yourself! For this you deserve a present.'

'Thank you,' Pnina said, and took a cinnamon-flavoured biscuit from Mrs Greenberg's floury fingers. 'I'll eat it while I'm walking.'

Pnina never meant to break her promise to her mother. She had planned to go straight back along the main street, looking into all the familiar shop-windows. She never knew exactly what it was that made her turn her head to the right, but something, some light, flashed at the very edge of her vision and she looked down the tiny alleyway and saw the golden windows. Later, she realized that it must have been the sun, now a little lower in the sky, striking every pane of glass on that side of the street, but at the time it seemed to her as though a fiery apricot light were pouring out of every house, beckoning her, saying: *come*. Come and look into all these golden windows and see what you will find. She began to walk along the pavement. At first, she was disappointed. Close to, the panes of glass were no longer golden, and what shops there were, hidden among these tall, ancient-looking houses, turned out to be dusty and neglected. There was a cobbler's with a window full of broken shoes waiting to be mended, and a watchmaker's shop where one antique clock was on display, blanketed with beige dust.

'I should go home now,' Pnina said to herself, and then she saw it. It was a window that seemed to have in it everything beautiful that was in the world. She could see sheets piled up in it, and embroidered pillowslips and tablecloths edged with frills of lace. There were petticoats and blouses hanging up and lying down. In one corner there was a heap of plump, satiny cushions and shawls and small rugs patterned with triangles and squares and wavy lines in scarlet and deep blue and purple and yellow and black. There was a piece of white velvet with rings and bracelets scattered all over it, and right at the front of the window, smiling out into the street, was a family of wooden dolls, each one smaller than the next, wearing head-scarves and flowered aprons painted in colours so bright that they sang out to Pnina through the glass. As soon as she saw them, Pnina knew that she should buy them as a present for Miriam's birthday. Miriam would love them. She would go in and ask how much they cost. She opened the door and stepped into the dimness of the shop.

At first, Pnina thought that she had walked into the window by mistake. There were so many things pushed into the room, piled into the corners and hanging from all the walls that she found it difficult to know exactly where to stand. At least there hadn't been any furniture in the window. Here, there were tables inlaid with mother-of-pearl, brass trays, marble ornaments, pottery vases, woven baskets, copper coffeepots, and on every flat surface, more linen: crocheted bedspreads, more sheets, more pillowslips, and enough tablecloths for every table in Jerusalem. From the ceiling hung a variety of lamps and lanterns. Pnina looked around. There must be someone here whom she could ask about the dolls. She peered into the corners, and at last saw someone – a woman squashed into a small armchair.

'Excuse me,' said Pnina, and the woman said:

'How can I help you, little girl?'

As soon as she spoke, Pnina wanted to run away. This is not a proper shop, she thought. The golden windows made me come here, drew me here. Hansel and Gretel were enchanted by all the sweets and gingerbread that the witch's house was made of, and I've been made to come in here by those dolls. I've been made to come into a witch's shop. Pnina shivered. The old woman, who had left her chair and was coming closer and closer to her, was smiling, and because of her smile, because of her teeth, she had become the most terrifying person Pnina had ever seen. She had thin white hair pulled into a twist at the back of her head, and her pink scalp showed through the strands here and there. She was wrinkled. Her eyes were blue and watery. Her body was large and lumpy in places and covered in a black dress. But the teeth! Pnina knew she would have nightmares about them every night. They were broken and browny-yellow and there were horrible gaps between them, and some were longer than others, and one even stuck out over the old lady's lower lip when she shut her mouth. In order not to see such a dreadful sight, Pnina looked down and then she saw the hands that were nearly as hideous as the teeth: misshapen, twisted fingers covered in brownish blotches and speckles so that they looked like two old vegetables left behind on a market stall, or two tree roots, hanging out of the long, black sleeves of the dress.

'I only wanted to know how much the dolls were. The family of dolls in the window.'

'I will call my sister, Natalya,' said the witch. 'She is the one who deals with the prices. Natalya!'

She opened her mouth wider to shout, so that Pnina could see more of her teeth. What would the witch's sister be like?

'I'm coming,' said a voice from far away, and then a small door opened right at the back of the shop and a fat woman with a great deal of frizzy grey hair came to stand next to the witch.

'Natalya, dear, this child is asking the price of the dolls.'

Natalya's eyes shone dark in a face like a ball of uncooked dough. Her fingers looked puffy and white and over her grey dress she wore a flowered apron. At least her teeth are normal, thought Pnina, and then realized how late she was going to be.

'I have to hurry now,' she said. 'My mother is expecting me at home, but I would like to know the price of the dolls.'

'Twenty-five piastres,' said Natalya, and the witch nodded, as though she'd thought as much, all along.

'I will bring the money next week,' Pnina said, and turned to go. As she reached the door, she called over her shoulder: 'Thank you!'

The sisters were gazing after her. They seemed to be sorry she was leaving. Maybe they expected her to buy the dolls now. I wish I had the money, Pnina thought. Maybe they don't think I'll come back. They look so sad.

'I will come back,' Pnina shouted. 'I love those dolls so much.'

She ran down the little alleyway towards the main road. The sun had moved on through the afternoon, and every window that had been brimming with gold was now a black square in the shadow of the buildings.

All the way home, Pnina thought about the dolls and how she wanted to keep them, and not give them to Miriam at all. Miriam, Pnina said to herself, will be four years old. She won't really mind what she gets . . . but she'd love those dolls. Anyone would . . . but Miriam would perhaps love something else just as much. I could give her my brooch in the shape of a heart . . . no, she might prick her fingers . . . well, there's the locket with space for a picture . . . but what would Mother say? She gave it to me last year. Pnina kicked the toes of her shoes along the pavement, cross because the only possible present for her sister was that beautiful set of dolls. She couldn't even buy the dolls and look around for something else for Miriam, because twenty piastres was all the money she had in the world, and although Zehava would give her five piastres towards Miriam's gift, she certainly wouldn't be able to afford more; and in any case, even if she were the richest woman in the world, money to buy a birthday present was meant for that purpose. You weren't supposed to spend all but a tiny bit of it on yourself. Pnina sighed. She was nearly at home. Soon it would be the Sabbath and candles would be lit and yellow light would fill every window in Jerusalem. Pnina loved Friday evenings, with everyone freshly bathed and wearing their best clothes to greet the day of rest, and the smell of especially delicious food filling the house. She began to feel a little more cheerful. Perhaps, she thought, stepping into the courtyard of her building and glancing up towards her mother's kitchen window, perhaps if Miriam has the dolls, it will be almost the same as having them myself. Maybe she will let me play with them. Climbing the stairs, she felt her heart heavy inside her like a small rock, and she knew it wouldn't be the same at all. Pnina wanted those dolls all to herself. She wanted to keep them on the shelf above her bed. She wanted no one else to touch them without her permission. She wanted to give them their names: special, magic names which only she, Pnina, would use. She knew that if she named them, they would come alive for her, they would become real people. If they were Miriam's, however often she was allowed to play with them, they would always be small wooden dolls, and nothing more.

'Wherever have you been, child?' Zehava cried, wiping her hands on her apron as she ran out of the kitchen. She'd been frying fish, Pnina knew, because her hands were white from the flour and a sharp, golden-brown fragrance hung in the air.

'I'm sorry, Mother,' Pnina said. 'I would have come sooner, but I found such a shop! I've never seen such a shop. In the window there are so many things, you think the glass is going to break.'

Zehava laughed. 'It can only be the shop belonging to the Arlozoroff sisters! Did you see them? Olga and Natalya? They must be ancient now, poor creatures.'

'Yes,' said Pnina. 'They are. The one called Olga looks like a witch. But they were very nice to me and they have a present that's just right for Miriam. I'm going to buy it next week.'

'You can tell me about such things later. Now it's time to get ready and you're not even bathed yet . . . run, child or the sun will set in the sky, and the Sabbath will be here before you've finished.'

Pnina ran. As she waited for her mother to fill the tin bath with warm water, a thought came into her mind. She looked at her mother.

'Why did you call them "poor creatures"?' she asked. 'If I had a shop filled with all those treasures, I'd think I was the luckiest person in the world.'

'They're all alone,' said Zehava. 'Just the two of them, in that poky little room behind the shop. That's what I meant. Really I should invite them one Friday evening. It's always a blessed thing to have guests to share your Friday meal.'

'Then come with me next week, and I'll show you Miriam's present and you can invite them.'

'Maybe,' said Zehava. 'We'll see what's happening next week. Maybe I'll come with you . . . now will you kindly get into this water, and leave gossiping about the Arlozoroffs for another time?'

Pnina stepped into the bath. She was trying to calculate how long it would take her to save another twenty-five piastres, and then, what if the dolls she had seen were the only ones? She tried to remember if there were any others in the shop at all. I can't remember seeing any, she thought, but in that crowded place they might have been hidden under something. Sitting as still as she could while Zehava scrubbed her back, Pnina thought: only six more days and then I'll see them again, pouring their colours out of the golden window of that little shop. I wish the time would go quickly. I wish it would.

Pnina had never lived through such a slow week in her life before. The days stretched and stretched through more hours than seemed bearable, and the nights were filled with dreams, but at last Friday came and it was time for Pnina to fetch the bread again.

'And will you come with me, Mother?' she asked for the thousandth time that week, 'And invite the Arlozoroffs? You promised.'

Zehava laughed. 'You forced me! You nagged me into it. Never have I seen such a persistent child. But you're right. I said I would invite them, so you can ask them if they'd like to come next week.'

'Oh, no!' Pnina cried. '*I* can't ask them. You said you would. I'd never dare to ask them. I'd be frightened.'

'Frightened of what, silly goose? They'll be delighted. Who asks them, after all, to go any-where? You'll be doing them a favour.'

'No,' said Pnina. 'I can't ask them. If you're not

coming with me, then you must send a letter. A proper invitation.'

'Who's got time to write letters with four rooms to clean before lunch?'

'I'll get you the paper,' said Pnina. 'I know exactly where it is.'

Zehava sat down at the table. 'Very well,' she said. 'To put a stop to your ceaseless nagging, I will do anything. Bring me the paper, and also a pen and ink. Anyone would think I was inviting the Queen of Sheba and her sister!'

As she approached the shop, Pnina began to run. There was the alley, and yes, there at the top on the right hand side, with the sun shining on to it, turning it into a sheet of gold, was the window of the Arlozoroffs' shop. Pnina walked up to it and looked in, and suddenly the whole world turned dark. The dolls had gone. Pnina felt tears filling her eyes and spilling over to run down her cheeks. This was something she had never imagined, not even for one second. Someone else had come and bought them, the dolls that should have been hers, and couldn't be, but which at least would have been in her house where she could look at them. She very nearly turned and ran away, but then she remembered her mother's invitation and how she had promised to deliver it. She had to go into the shop.

The witch-like sister, Olga, was sitting in her armchair almost as though she hadn't moved at all since the previous week.

'Good day, child,' she said and stood up, and

began to walk towards Pnina. 'Oh, it's you . . . the little girl who asked the price of the dolls.'

Hearing the old lady mention them made Pnina hurt all over. She sank down on to a small wooden stool that happened to be positioned near the counter, and started to howl and sob. The old lady put her hands to her head.

'Natalya! Natalya come quickly! There's a child here crying. Natalya, what shall we do?'

Natalya bustled in from the back room.

'It's her,' Olga said. 'The child who wanted the dolls.' Natalya knelt down beside Pnina.

'What's the matter dear?' she said gently. 'Have you perhaps lost your money?'

'Oh, no,' Pnina sniffed and rummaged in her pocket to find the handkerchief in which her money was safely tied. 'I've wrapped it up. Only now I need the handkerchief for my nose because I'm crying so much, and I don't need the money.'

'Why not?' asked Natalya. 'Have you changed your mind about the dolls?'

Pnina shook her head. 'No,' she said. 'I haven't changed my mind . . . but they've gone! I've waited a whole week to buy them and they're not here any longer. Some other child has them and I'll never see them again.'

'No, no,' said Olga. 'They're not in the window because we kept them for you. After you left last week, I said: "We must put those aside for that child. If someone else buys them, she will be most upset." They're in the back room. Come now, dry your eyes and have a short rest in our room to recover.'

'Perhaps,' said Natalya 'you will drink a glass of cordial, while we wrap them up.'

Pnina could feel her sadness disappearing as the sisters spoke. It was as though a thick, woollen blanket of misery which had been covering her up was suddenly lifted off, and thrown away. She flung her arms round Olga, who was standing right next to her.

'Oh, thank you! Thank you for keeping them! I love them so much! I'm so happy now. I feel as if I'll never cry again. Can we go and get them, please?'

'Certainly,' said Natalya. 'Follow me. Olga will wrap them up, and I will fetch you a drink and perhaps some sugared almonds.'

The room at the back of the shop was the darkest place Pnina had ever seen. The tables and chairs were made of wood that looked almost black, and there was a black cupboard with carved doors towering in the corner. All over the walls were framed pictures of ladies and gentlemen in old-fashioned clothes and strange furry hats. There was one photograph of a baby in a lacy shawl.

'Is that your baby?' Pnina asked, pointing.

'No,' Olga answered. 'My youngest sister. Not Natalya. The youngest one.'

'Does she live here too?'

'She died,' Olga said. 'When she was about your age.'

'Was she ill?' Pnina wanted to know.

'No . . . she was . . . we were all in a pogrom. A very terrible thing is a pogrom.'

Pnina shivered. Even the word frightened her.

'What is it?' she whispered.

'It is when bad people attack others . . . burn their houses, kill them as they are running away . . . even little children they kill. Natalya and I were the only ones left in our family, so we ran away to here. To Jerusalem.' Seeing Pnina's face, the old woman smiled. 'These are not good things for you to hear. Let us wrap the dolls and forget those horrors from days long ago.' She opened a drawer in the sideboard and took out the largest of the dolls and set her on the table. Pnina stretched out a hand to touch the glossy paint on her head.

'She's so beautiful,' she said, 'but where are the others, the smaller ones?' A terrifying thought struck her. What if the dolls were twenty-five piastres each and she could only afford to buy one? But Olga was smiling.

'You do not know? You have never seen dolls like this before?' She took it in her hands and twisted it, as though she were wringing out a piece of washing. The doll split into two parts, and Pnina saw a smaller one inside. Olga took the second doll out, opened it to reveal the third one, and then the smallest doll appeared in her turn and smiled at all the others.

'Then,' said Olga, 'you put each one back together again like this . . . and you have four dolls. And when you are ready to pack them away, they go one inside the other again.'

'Oh, that's wonderful,' Pnina breathed. 'It's the most wonderful surprise. I love them so much.'

Natalya had come into the room and was pouring a red drink into tall glasses.

'You said they were for your sister's birthday,' she said, and added: 'Here, take a drink and a sweet.'

The sugared almonds lay like pale, prettily-coloured pebbles in a china dish. Pnina chose a mauve one, and said: 'They *are* for Miriam's birthday. I wish they could be mine, but I can't afford two sets, and I can't even afford to buy them for myself and get another present for Miriam. I've thought and thought about it the whole week, and I've decided that if Miriam has them then at least they will be in my house and perhaps she'll let me play with them sometimes.'

'You are a kind child,' said Olga. 'Take another sugared almond. Take a pink one. I always liked the pink ones best, because they are the colour of pink blossoms, but now of course, my days of eating sugared almonds are over. All my teeth would certainly fall out!' She cackled, looking more like a witch than ever and Pnina was glad to be able to concentrate on the sweets and not have to gaze at that mouth.

'Oh,' she said suddenly. 'I nearly forgot. I have a letter for you both from my mother.'

'A letter?' said Natalya. 'Do we know your mother?'

'My mother is Zehava Genzel,' said Pnina, and at once both Olga and Natalya began to flutter and squawk around the table like a pair of ancient chickens. Natalya squawked loudest.

'Well, my goodness! Imagine . . . what a small world! Zehava Genzel! Oh, her mother (your grandmother, blessed be her memory), was such a wonderful woman . . . and we knew your mother when she was like you. Olga, doesn't the child remind you of her grandmother, now that you know who she is?'

'Of course, of course . . . I knew she was a special

child. How lovely! All these years . . . your mother used to like our shop when she was about your age. And now she is writing to us. Just imagine! What a happy day!'

The two women seemed content to pass the sealed envelope backwards and forwards over the table, smoothing it as though it were a beloved pet, admiring it as though it were a priceless jewel, and showing no curiosity at all about what it might say. Pnina, even though she knew what her mother had written, was growing more and more impatient. It was difficult to interrupt the flow of delighted chatter, but at last Olga and Natalya paused for breath, and she said quickly:

'Don't you want to know what's *in* the letter? Aren't you going to read it?'

'I suppose so,' said Olga. 'But no one ever writes us a real letter . . . only bills of sale and business things . . . very boring . . . so this is a real treat for us. We are enjoying it.'

'But the child has to go home, Olga,' said Natalya. 'Open it now and let us see what it says. We may have to send an answer with . . .' Natalya's hand flew to her mouth. 'What a disgrace, little one! We haven't even asked your name. How rude we are!'

'It doesn't matter,' Pnina said. 'My name is Pnina.'

'Lovely,' said Olga. 'Perfect! Pnina . . . a pearl. It suits you very well.'

Pnina smiled, but noticed that her mother's letter was still sealed.

'Thank you,' she said, and looked pointedly at the envelope.

'We still haven't opened it,' said Natalya. 'I will fetch the letter-knife.'

By the time the letter-knife was found in a drawer in the sideboard, by the time it had been polished with a corner of the tablecloth to remove every possible speck, by the time Olga had located her reading spectacles behind a bowl filled with dusty-looking fruit, another ten minutes had passed. Then at long last, Zehava's sheet of paper was unfolded and Olga read the letter aloud.

'Well!' said Natalya, when she had heard it. 'I'm quite overwhelmed. Such a kind invitation . . . how very exciting. Olga, we must answer at once. Where is the paper? The pen and ink?' Pnina could imagine the minutes and minutes that writing an answer would take. She said:

'Oh, no, please . . . my mother said you were not to worry about replying with a letter. I will take your answer back with me.'

Olga nodded. 'It is typical of such a fine person as your mother that she would spare us the least bit of trouble. How kind she is! How we are both longing to see her! Tell her we will be there next Friday at six o'clock, and that we are most honoured. Now we must wrap the dolls up and send you home, or your mother will wonder what has befallen you.'

'And then,' said Pnina, 'they took ages and ages finding the right kind of tissue paper to wrap the dolls in. Everything took *so* long.'

'Never mind,' said Zehava. 'We've given them a little pleasure in their lives. I will prepare a really nice meal for them, poor things.'

'With nothing too hard to bite on,' said Pnina. 'Olga's teeth are broken.' She shuddered.

'Oh, nothing too hard,' Zehava smiled. 'I won't even put any nuts in the strudel. Now take those dolls and go and hide them away where Miriam won't see them. It was clever of you to find such a wonderful present. I'm surprised you don't want to keep them for yourself.'

'I'll go and hide them,' said Pnina. 'Somewhere where they'll be safe till Tuesday.'

Preparations for the Friday meal began early on Thursday morning.

'What a week!' said Zehava, as she minced fish and chopped vegetables. 'First Miriam's birthday and now this.'

Pnina, Sarah, and Leah were helping in the kitchen. The boys had been sent to fetch water and buy firewood. Little Miriam was sitting under the table with the set of dolls that Pnina had given her. They had been her very favourite present.

'Will we be ready in time?' asked Sarah.

'Yes, of course,' said Zehava. 'I'm only making a few extra things.'

But on Friday evening, it seemed to Pnina that the whole kitchen was bursting with gefilte fish, and mashed-up potatoes, and tureens of fragrant chicken soup, and different kinds of cakes, all without nuts so that Olga could eat them.

When the Arlozoroff sisters arrived, they were wearing their grandest clothes: leather gloves and fur coats over their dresses, and lace collars fastened with amber brooches and elegant hats pushed down to their eyebrows.

'Welcome!' said Zehava. 'It is so many years since I've seen you, but you both look just the same.'

'You are lying, of course,' said Olga, 'but we forgive you. How like your dear mother you look! And all these beautiful children! Pnina we know, of course, but all these others . . . how splendid! And this must be little Miriam, the birthday girl.'

Miriam ran to hide in Zehava's skirts. Taking their coats off, and settling down at the table seemed to Pnina to go on for a very long time. At last, though, the meal began. The food lay on the white tablecloth, the candlelight played on every face and threw shadows on to the wall, the wine sparkled in the best glasses.

'It is very many years,' said Olga, 'since we have had an evening as pleasant as this.'

Pnina, who had been only half-listening to the grown-ups talk about the old days, heard the remark and immediately thought of the shop. She thought of Olga and Natalya, hidden from everyone behind a high wall of linen and jewellery and furniture and ornaments, hidden in a small back room where dark cupboards loomed over them, and where the only people they ever saw were hanging on the wall in silver frames.

'When Pnina came into our little room,' Olga

was saying, just as though she had been reading Pnina's thoughts, 'I think she was the first visitor we'd had since last year. Such a wonderful treat!'

'I will come to see you every week,' said Pnina. 'When I go and fetch the bread.'

'And me,' Miriam piped up. 'Pnina take Miriam!'

'Of course,' said Natalya. 'You should all come.'

'But not all at once,' said Olga. 'There would not be room in the shop. We have too much stock!' She smiled. 'It is because not many people buy from us, but we . . . we can't resist anything beautiful. We have to have it, so we buy it and put it in the window, which gets more and more full. One day the whole shop will explode and all our things will fly through the air and the whole of Jerusalem will be draped in our linen, and our jewellery will be scattered among the paving-stones.'

When the meal was over, Pnina stood up. 'I have to put Leah and Miriam to bed now,' she said to Olga and Natalya. 'So I must say goodnight.' As she spoke, she thought that perhaps her mother would tell her to kiss them both. She shivered. The teeth . . . well, she would close her eyes and hold her breath and kiss Olga's cheek very quickly and it would soon be over.

'But Pnina,' said Natalya, 'you must wait and open your present.'

'It isn't my birthday till June,' said Pnina.

'Nevertheless,' said Olga, 'we have brought presents. Sugared almonds for all the children, and some handkerchiefs for you, Zehava, and this small gift for Pnina.' She burrowed in her handbag, and handed the sweets to Sarah and a packet to Zehava. For Pnina there was a small cardboard box.

'Thank you,' said Pnina, thinking: now I really *will* have to kiss them. Whatever can this be?

Inside, the box was filled with tissue paper . . . but there was something hard . . . something rounded . . . a doll . . . a doll like Miriam's. Pnina pulled the tissue away.

'Oh! Oh! I can't believe it. Are they really for me? Really? They're beautiful. So beautiful . . . even lovelier than Miriam's. Oh, I love you!' Pnina ran to Olga and Natalya and kissed them and hugged them, one after the other. 'This is the best present I've ever had.'

Pnina opened the biggest doll and took the others out and lined them up on the table for everyone to admire.

'This one I shall call Olga, after you,' she said, 'and the next one Natalya.'

The two old ladies smiled.

'Now,' said Pnina, 'I need two more Russian names.'

'Our mother was Sonya,' said Olga. 'That's a pretty name.'

'And the littlest one can be Tamara,' said Natalya.

Pnina knew as soon as Natalya had spoken that Tamara was the name of the baby in the photograph, the one in the lacy dress, the one who had been killed long ago in a pog-something. Pnina had forgotten the word, but she remembered the baby's face. She looked at the two old ladies, both suddenly very quiet and saw that their eyes glittered in the light of the candles as though they were filled with tears.

Pnina found it hard to fall asleep that night. The dolls, Olga, Natalya, Sonya and little Tamara were lined up in the dark. She could see the shapes they made against the wall. Leah was asleep, and not moving. Miriam was snuffling and snorting in her cot. Pnina got out of bed and went to the window. She wasn't the only person in the city who was awake so late. Here and there, there were places where a candle still flickered; there were still some golden windows in the darkness of the night.

A GARDEN WITH RABBITS 1912

'I know just what Pnina meant,' Harry said. 'Sometimes I look out of our apartment and I can see the lights shining in the windows of all the other apartments in the block opposite ours and I wonder who lives there and what they're doing. I've seen dolls like that, too. You have one, on the sideboard in the other room. I used to play with it when I was small.'

'That's the same one,' Aunt Rachel smiled. 'Pnina gave her set of dolls to me, because she never had any children of her own. I don't know what happened to Miriam's. Did you ever look round your grandmother's house, when she was alive?'

'No,' said Harry. 'I guess I was too small.'

'Then we'll never know what became of them. Never mind. I'll tell you a story about Miriam now. Well, about Pnina and Miriam really, and you will meet your grandfather as a boy not much older than you.'

*   *   *

'Why does it always have to be me?' Pnina said. 'Why can't anyone else take Miriam out for her walk?'

'You know very well,' said Zehava, 'that everyone else is busy. The boys have gone to help Uncle
Ezra in the shop, Sarah is making Haman's ears
with me ready for Purim, and Leah has gone to
spend the day with Rachel.'

'I could make Haman's ears instead of Sarah,'
Pnina suggested. Haman's ears were the triangular
cakes filled with honey and poppyseeds that everybody ate at Purim, when they dressed up in fancy
dress costumes, and remembered the story of brave
Queen Esther and the wicked Haman, who died in
the end as a punishment for his evildoing.

'Eating the cakes you are good at and you enjoy,'
Zehava laughed. 'But making them has always
bored you. That's what you say when I call you to
help me in the kitchen. To pick up a dishcloth and
dry a fork is for you a big achievement. I should
have thought you'd much rather walk about Jerusalem, especially on such a beautiful day.'

'I don't mind walking,' said Pnina, and it was
true. Of all the Genzel children, Pnina knew the
city best: the wide roads winding down the hill,
the buildings made of yellow stones that glittered
in the sun, and the narrow streets where tall houses
with shuttered windows cast deep cool shadows
even when the sun was at its fiercest.

'Then what *do* you mind?' her mother asked.

'Having to listen to Miriam's questions every
single minute. Do you know, she can hardly manage
to breathe properly, she talks so much. She wants to
know everything. It's exhausting. Also, she never
wants to come where I want to take her. She wants

to look at the shops, or else go down past the hospital, or else up to the market.'

'And where would you go?'

'I like all the little streets. I like the quiet places where not many people go. I like looking at all the windows and imagining who lives there. Miriam says that's boring.'

Zehava said: 'As a special favour to you, then, I shall tell Miriam that you are both to go wherever *you* decide, and if she complains, you are to bring her straight home. Will that do?'

'I suppose so,' said Pnina. 'I'll go and get ready. If we're going, we may as well set out. Will you keep a bit of the poppyseed mixture for me to taste when I come home?'

'Can't you wait till Purim comes?'

'No,' said Pnina. 'I want a taste today. I'm sure that's the only reason Sarah has agreed to help you. She can have little tastes of everything as she works.'

Zehava laughed. 'Those little tastes are a cook's reward for making lovely food for everyone, but I notice it's never been enough to tempt you into the kitchen.'

'But today you will keep me a little, won't you? As a reward for listening to Miriam all afternoon?'

'Just a teaspoonful,' said Zehava, 'and you'd better go soon, or the day will have become night. I'll find Miriam now and get her ready.'

'And tell her she has to obey me completely. Go exactly where I want her to go for a change.'

'I will bribe her with a teaspoonful of poppyseed

and honey. She is almost as greedy as you are.'

'Can we go this way now?' Miriam asked. 'Please, Pnina, we've been walking along your streets for hours and hours and there hasn't been a single shop. I've only seen six people the whole afternoon and three of them have been very old men who don't count at all.'

'So who *does* count?' Pnina thought she'd never heard such nonsense in her life. Whatever went on in her little sister's head?

'Ladies count,' said Miriam, 'especially if they have hats on, and handsome young men and babies. They're the best. Can we go this way now? There's a shop that sells jewels down there, I know there is. We went past it once with Mother on our way to the dressmaker's, but she wouldn't stop.'

'You're thinking of some other street,' said Pnina. 'This is nowhere near where Eva lives.'

'It is! I'm sure it is! Let's at least go and have a look.'

'No,' said Pnina, 'I don't want to go down there. I want to go this way.'

'Well, I don't.'

'It doesn't matter what you want. Mother said you had to obey me.'

'I've obeyed you for hours.'

'You have to keep obeying me till we get home.'

'Then,' said Miriam, 'I want to go home now and stop obeying. I don't like it.'

'I don't care,' said Pnina. 'Because I say we're not going home yet. I want to go down this street.'

'I'm going to sulk,' Miriam announced, pulling her pretty round face into what she hoped was a dreadful, fierce scowl. 'I'm going to sulk till we get home. I shan't say a single word to you. I'll stop talking to you. That'll be your punishment.'

'How lovely!' said Pnina. 'My ears could do with the rest. Chatter, chatter, chatter, that's all you do all day long. A bit of silence will come as a pleasant relief.' Miriam snorted, and followed her sister.

She won't be able to keep up this silence till we get home, Pnina thought. Especially if I keep talking to her. In the end she'll just have to answer, or she'll burst. And I'm going to go on talking, oh yes! I'm not having her telling Mother I didn't say a word. I shall be completely normal and friendly. Miriam will have nothing to complain about. I shall make up stories about the people in these houses to amuse her. Pnina looked at her sister, whose nose was pointed towards the sky in a way that said very clearly: 'Do whatever you like. It's no business of mine.'

'Miriam,' she said. 'Bring your nose down from up there and enjoy this street. There are some very exciting people living here.' The nose remained fixed on the heavens. 'Not everyone knows this, because it looks like an ordinary street, but it isn't. It isn't at all. It's a very special street. Shall I tell you who lives in this house, for instance?'

The upturned nose gave a haughty sniff. Well, thought Pnina, I know she's listening. Probably she's bursting to ask me all kinds of questions. Let me think of some really fantastical tales . . .

'In that house, there lives a woman who turns into a bear every evening. Truly. She can't help it. Her children have to make sure she never goes out at night. They never tell anyone, and try to keep her indoors after dark, of course, but once she left the house in the evening and I happened to see her. She won't hurt us now. It's daylight and she looks quite normal. In fact, she wouldn't even hurt us at night. She's a very friendly sort of bear and her family are all devoted to her, but still, I don't think I'd like to see her again. The very worst thing of all was those big, hairy paws in lacy gloves . . . ugh!' Pnina gave an elaborate shudder. She glanced at Miriam, whose nose was definitely lower by a couple of inches. What's more, she wasn't slouching and dragging along the pavement: she was walking quite briskly. She doesn't want to miss a word of what I'm saying, Pnina thought. I'd better not stop.

'Here,' she said, 'there lives a man whose arms

and legs are made of wood. He looks all right from the outside, so that you could never tell, but he was very badly hurt one day when he fell off his horse, and they had to give him specially carved wooden arms and legs. He walks a little stiffly, naturally, and wears his sleeves extra long to hide his arms and most of his hands, but otherwise he's just like anyone else. There's a special hospital he went to in Vienna where they make wooden limbs. They're all hanging in this huge room, rows and rows of arms and legs in all shapes and sizes, and if you are hurt, all you have to do is go to the hospital and choose . . . it's almost as easy as buying shoes or gloves.'

As she spoke, Pnina was so carried away by the story of the man with wooden arms and legs that she walked along without really paying attention to where she was. In the maze of tiny, twisted streets that lay behind the huge magnificence of the Russian Orthodox Church, she turned first along a road that went to the left, then down another tempting street with Miriam following behind her, listening, until at last the girls found themselves in a long, sloping road where a cool silence lay over the stones and there was no visible sign of people. The girls walked and walked and at last, Pnina finished the story and turned to see how her sister was enjoying it, but Miriam was no longer keeping up with her. She was about fifty yards away, standing at a tall gate made of iron curled into elaborate patterns, which Pnina had vaguely noticed out of the corner of her eye as she passed it.

'Miriam!' Pnina called. 'Come here this minute! What are you doing? It's rude to look so hard into people's gates like that.' As she spoke, Pnina retraced her steps to where her little sister stood on tiptoe, with her head almost through the metal railings. Miriam turned as she approached. All the scowls had disappeared and instead she looked like a picture of the sun drawn by a child: happy and bright and with a smile so wide it stretched from one side of her face to the other.

'Pnina, look!' she said. 'Look what I've found!'

'Aah! So we've finished sulking then, have we?'

'Sulking's stupid,' said Miriam. 'This is so lovely. Come and see. Oh, you're clever, Pnina. You knew this garden was here all the time, didn't you? You wanted it to be a surprise. Thank you.'

Pnina came to stand beside her sister. She, too, peered through the metal railings. She saw a quiet courtyard, with a small fountain in the centre surrounded by white flagstones. All around the fountain there were enormous pottery urns filled with new flowers, just opening for the spring, and in one corner, a tree with white blossom rose almost as high as the balcony. There were other trees in the courtyard as well: small palms and pepper trees and little cypress trees, also in pots. There were cacti growing in one corner and in another . . .

'Pnina,' said Miriam, 'look over there. Can you see? There are rabbits.'

'Oh, yes,' said Pnina. 'I can see them. I can see a black and white one and a white one. Oh, they're so beautiful!'

'Let's go in,' Miriam said. 'Let's go in there and look at them.'

'We can't,' Pnina said. 'This is someone's house. We can't possibly just march in there and stroke the rabbits.'

'Why not?'

'We can't, that's all.'

'But we won't hurt them,' Miriam begged. 'Please, Pnina, just for a moment. We'll just touch them for a minute and then go . . . and look how quiet it is. Maybe everyone has gone out.'

Pnina sighed. 'I suppose there isn't any harm.' She, too, wanted a closer look at the rabbits, and Miriam was hopping up and down with excitement.

'Come on, then, just for a second.' Pnina tried to push down the latch on the metal gate, but it refused to move. Then she noticed a keyhole and looked at it carefully.

'The gate is locked, Miriam. We can't go in. I'm so sorry.'

Miriam sighed. 'Will you bring me again tomorrow?'

'Yes,' said Pnina, 'I'll bring you again, but now I think we should go home.'

'Yes,' said Miriam.

Pnina wasn't quite sure of the way home, but she had no intention of telling her younger sister. I will find it, she thought. If I turn left here, and start walking uphill, then eventually I will come to somewhere I recognize. The girls walked and walked, and at last arrived at the florist's shop, just down the road from where they lived. Pnina felt safe again. She turned to her sister.

'You haven't been speaking much,' she said. 'I thought sulking was over.'

'I haven't been sulking,' Miriam answered. 'I've been thinking about those rabbits.'

'Yes,' Pnina said. 'So have I.'

This wasn't entirely true. Pnina had been worrying. Firstly she had worried about finding the way home, and now that they were nearly there, another, even greater worry filled all her thoughts. She had promised to take Miriam back to visit the rabbits next day, and she didn't think she could remember how to reach the house. Down to the Russian Orthodox Church, and then was it left or right? And whatever would Miriam say if she could never find them again? Pnina went on worrying about this on and off for the rest of the day and far into the night. Everyone else had gone to sleep long ago, but Pnina lay awake retracing – trying to retrace – in her mind the paths she had taken earlier in the day.

'What do you mean, you don't know where they are?' Miriam's brow was darkening, her mouth beginning to turn down at the corners. 'You promised me yesterday to bring me back to see the rabbits. Why didn't you say *then* that you wouldn't be able to find them?'

'Well,' Pnina searched around desperately for an excuse. 'Yesterday I thought I *would* be able to find them, but now I can't.'

'Can't we look for them a bit longer?' Miriam

asked, her voice wobbling dangerously.

'No,' said Pnina. 'We have to go home now.'

'I don't *want* to go home,' Miriam shouted. 'I want to find those rabbits. You said we could.'

'I want to find them too,' Pnina shouted back. 'Just as much as you do. There's no need to get in a temper about it. That doesn't help anyone.'

'I don't care! I don't care! I want to see them,' Miriam shrieked. Pnina sighed, and looked around anxiously. Thank goodness there's no one in the street, she thought. I must get her home quickly. Miriam's tantrums were famous in the building where the Genzels lived. They broke over the house like thunderstorms: noisy, dark, wet and frightening, but like storms, they didn't last long and her brothers and sisters had long ago learned that the best way to get through them was simply to wait until they had worn themselves out. That's all very well at home, thought Pnina, as she took her little sister's hand and began to drag her through the streets. Out here in the open, if anyone sees me, goodness knows what they'll think. Maybe they'll think I've been hitting her. Maybe I *should* hit her. Perhaps it'll stop her wailing. Pnina pulled Miriam behind her, quickened her step and nearly broke into a run in her anxiety to reach the safety of her own house. She turned into a road that sloped upwards and looked around her. Was this, could this possibly be, the right way? She sighed. She was so eager to get Miriam away from prying eyes that she had almost forgotten to notice where they were. The street was empty, but, Pnina thought, that didn't mean that people weren't staring out of their windows, using the edges of their curtains to hide behind. Miriam's howls were quieter now. She was out of breath from keeping up with her sister, because it is difficult to howl and run at the same time. Instead of howling, Miriam had turned to sniffing and loud sighing. Then, suddenly, Pnina stopped.

'Miriam,' she whispered. 'I think I've found the house. Isn't this it? Look, there's the gate.'

'Oh!' Miriam was too overcome to speak. She gasped and looked through the railings. Yes, there was the black and white rabbit and his white brother, both pressing their noses against the wire netting of their hutch.

'They want to see us,' said Miriam. 'Look! The white one is standing on its back paws and waving its ears at us.' She jumped up and down and called out: 'Wait, little rabbits! We're coming! We're coming!'

'Ssh!' said Pnina. 'Do you have to announce it to the world? We're not supposed to be here, going into strange gardens, and anyway, the gate could still be locked, do you remember? I *did* tell you the gate could be locked, didn't I?'

'Yes,' said Miriam. Pnina looked a little less worried. At least there wouldn't be another tantrum-tempest if they couldn't get in. 'But you must at least try.'

'Very well,' said Pnina. She tried the gate and it was open. It wasn't until that very second that she realized how much she had been hoping that it would be closed. Miriam began squeaking loudly.

'Be quiet!' Pnina hissed. 'You sound like a mad mouse. And you'll have the whole household coming to see what the noise is if you're not careful.' She looked around the silent courtyard. Nothing stirred. Even the rabbits were quite motionless, apart from their little twitching noses.

'Come on,' Pnina whispered, and she stepped into the courtyard with Miriam following closely behind her. The girls tiptoed across the white flagstones, past the terracotta urns brimming with flowers under the scented fronds of the pepper tree, and over to the corner where the wooden hutch stood. As the girls came closer, the rabbits became quite excited.

'Maybe they think we're bringing them food,' said Pnina.

'We should have brought them some scraps from home,' said Miriam. 'Now they won't like us.'

'Of course they'll like us,' said Pnina. 'They look very fat to me. I'm sure whoever owns them looks after them very well.'

'Next time,' said Miriam, 'I will bring them some pieces of carrot.'

'Sssh,' said Pnina. 'Don't talk.' She wanted to change the subject. She had no intention of coming here again, and didn't know how to tell Miriam. Perhaps she would ask their mother to forbid it, then Miriam's storms of tears would have to be dealt with by someone else. She looked at her sister. Miriam had pushed her chubby forefinger through the wire netting and was stroking the black and white rabbit's nose. The white one seemed a little shy, a little unwilling to come forward and claim attention.

'Snowy,' Miriam whispered, trying to entice him. Snowy! Pnina thought. What a boring name for a white rabbit. Surely they could think of something better? Blossom? Star? Fluffy? She was pondering names when the voice boomed out from behind her.

'What are you girls doing, may I ask?' it said, and both Pnina and Miriam whirled round, terrified. The owner of the booming voice was enormous: a huge man with a long, black beard and a long black jacket. He was limping across the courtyard towards them, leaning on a walking stick. For one horrible moment, Pnina thought that her story about the man with wooden arms and legs had come true, but no, she could see, now that the man was very close to them, that his hands, anyway, were real. Real and hairy, covered with a kind of dark fur, almost to his fingernails. She shuddered and felt Miriam taking her hand and drawing closer. Perhaps this was a person who sometimes turned into a wolf. She spoke and her words sounded like the chirpings of a frightened bird.

'Please, sir, we're sorry. We are really doing no harm. My sister and I . . . we saw the rabbits yesterday, and as we were passing the house today . . . we thought that just one tiny stroke . . . wouldn't hurt anyone. My sister is so fond of animals.'

'Well,' said the man. 'No harm has been done, I suppose . . . but if I'd wanted children coming in from the streets to stroke the rabbits which belong to my son, then I would have had a sign hung outside, saying, "Zoological Gardens".' He thought that this remark was very amusing, and smiled, showing big, square, pale yellow teeth.

Pnina said again: 'We're sorry. We won't come back, I promise,' and she began to edge away slowly towards the gate.

'Then I shall say no more about it,' said the huge hairy man. 'Come, I will make sure to lock the gate after you.'

The turning of the key in the lock echoed in the stillness of the afternoon. Pnina and Miriam stood outside the gates, watching the man limp back towards the house, his stick tapping on the stones of the courtyard.

'He's gone,' said Miriam. 'I'm glad. He was really horrible. Wave goodbye to Snowy and Spotty.'

Spotty! That was even worse than Snowy. Surely they could find better names? Pnina was on the point of opening her mouth to say so, when she suddenly realized that they would never be seeing the rabbits again. At least she hadn't been the one to break the bad news.

'Can we go back tomorrow?' Miriam said, and Pnina sighed.

'No, Miriam. Didn't you understand what that man was saying? He said we mustn't come back. He said the rabbits belonged to his son.'

'He said,' Miriam smiled, 'that we mustn't go in. He didn't say we couldn't look from the gate.'

'But where's the pleasure in looking?' Pnina cried.

'We won't be able to touch the rabbits and you'll feel really upset in the end. I know you will.'

'Not "the rabbits",' said Miriam. 'Snowy and Spotty.'

'Why did you choose those names?' Pnina asked.

'Because,' said Miriam, smiling radiantly, 'I think they're lovely. Don't you think they're lovely names?'

Well, what difference does it make after all? Pnina thought. They're not our rabbits.

'Lovely names,' she said. 'It was clever of you to think of them.'

Miriam skipped along the pavement, all the way home.

The next day, Miriam was ill. She had felt, she said, 'wobbly and sore and hot' at lunchtime, and Zehava had put her to bed. All the children took turns to sit with her, and hold cloths wrung out in cold water over her forehead, and try and persuade her to drink the milk, or soup or juices that Zehava had prepared. Sometimes she tried a few drops, and from time to time she fell asleep, but when she was awake, she tossed and turned in her small bed, and her dark curls lay damp on her cheek, and her eyes were too bright. The doctor came and prescribed some green medicine, but Miriam refused to take it.

When it was Pnina's turn to sit with her, she told Miriam long stories about the adventures of Snowy and Spotty. The rabbits went to the seaside near Jaffa, they dressed up for Purim, they took a ride in a horse-drawn carriage to the hills outside the city. Pnina was trying so hard to think of new adventures that after a while her head was in a whirl. Then she noticed that two fat tears were sliding out of the corners of Miriam's eyes.

'What are you crying for?' Pnina asked. 'Don't you like my stories?'

'Yes, I like them, but they make me sad.'

'They're supposed to make you happy,' Pnina sighed. 'I'll stop if you don't like them.'

'I *do* like them, but I want to see the real rabbits. I want to stroke Snowy and Spotty. I really, really do.' Pnina had a sudden brilliant idea.

'Will you drink your medicine and all your soup and drinks and try very hard to get better if I promise you that you can stroke the rabbits?'

Miriam sat up in bed. 'Oh, yes, Pnina! I'll drink the whole bottle of medicine at one gulp.'

'Mother!' Pnina shouted, and Zehava came running in from the kitchen, wiping her hands on her apron. 'Mother, Miriam has promised me to drink all her drinks and take all her medicine and get better as quickly as she possibly can.'

'Thank God!' cried Zehava, and Pnina realized how many days it was since her mother had looked really happy. She also noticed the dark shadows under her mother's eyes. Pnina knew that Zehava sat next to Miriam's bed all through the night. It was no wonder she was tired.

'I'll go and fetch some chicken soup this very minute,' Zehava said. 'And the medicine.'

When she had left the room, Miriam asked: 'How will you manage it, Pnina? That hairy man told us not to come back.'

'Leave it to me,' said Pnina. 'I have an amazing secret plan.'

The next afternoon, Pnina walked alone through the maze of streets behind the Russian Orthodox Church. She knew the way a little better now. It's down here, she said to herself, and then right by that house with green shutters. I must make sure not to step on any cracks in the pavement. If I can do that, it'll be all right. Miriam will get better quickly, and we'll be allowed to visit the rabbits. She wished that what she had told Miriam about an amazing secret plan was really true. Without such a plan, Pnina didn't know what would happen when she reached the house. Or rather, she thought that she did know, and was very nervous indeed. She would have to ring the bell, ask to see the hairy man and tell him the whole story. Perhaps he only *looks* horrible and has a very kind heart, said Pnina to herself. But he threw us out the other day, so how kind can he be? She shook her head miserably. I'll just have to try my hardest. I shall tell him my sister has become ill from wanting to visit the rabbits. Maybe there's even some truth in that. She tiptoed over one crack, then another. Nearly there.

When she arrived at the house and looked through the railings, the hairy brute was nowhere to be seen. Instead, a skinny-looking boy with a long neck and sandy hair was standing next to the hutch. He had his back to her. This must be, Pnina thought, the hairy monster's son. He didn't look a bit frightening. What a miracle! And the rabbits actually belong to him. If he gives permission for them to be stroked, then what can anyone do to stop it?

'Hey!' Pnina called out. 'Excuse me! Hey! Could you please come over here a minute?' The boy whirled round to face her. He looked terrified. Pnina was intrigued. Why was this boy, who was about Eli's age, frightened of a younger girl?

'M – m – me?' he said, so quietly that Pnina could hardly hear him.

'Yes, you,' said Pnina. 'I'd like to talk to you, but it's difficult when you're standing right over there. Can you come here, please, to the gate?'

The boy made his way across the courtyard so slowly that Pnina nearly shouted out, 'I won't bite you', but then decided against it. She knew from observing her brothers that boys didn't like admitting they were scared. Instead, she called out as he drew closer, what she thought of as a friendly remark:

'Hello, what's your name?'

He was right beside the railings now. Pnina could have easily reached through the bars of the gate to touch him.

'D – D – D–D–D–David,' he said, and blushed crimson and looked at his feet.

'I'm Pnina,' she said, and realized why the poor boy had been so nervous about speaking to her. He had a bad stammer and clearly found it very hard to make conversation with people. Pnina wondered whether it would be rude to mention his stammer

or whether she had better pretend not to notice it. In the end she decided to speak her mind.

'Hello, David,' she said. 'It's a pleasure to meet you. I hope you don't mind speaking to me. I know it's a bit hard for you to answer, but I really don't mind waiting to hear what you say, so don't feel bad about it and blush every time you open your mouth.' She smiled, and to her surprise, David smiled back.

'W–w–w–why have you come b–b–ack?' he said. 'I s–s–aw you and your s–s–sister. M–m–my father d–d–doesn't want me to b–b–be embarrassed so he d–d–doesn't l–l–let many p–p–p–people come here. I h–h–h–aven't g–got many friends.' David seemed out of breath at the end of such a long sentence.

'We'll be your friends and we'd love to come and visit you,' Pnina said, quickly. 'My little sister's ill, and she likes your rabbits so much that I promised her to come and ask your father for permission to stroke them sometimes.'

'They're m–m–m–my rabbits,' David said. 'I g–g–give you permission. Will you t–t–t–talk to me when you c–c–come?'

'Yes, of course,' said Pnina. 'But hadn't you better ask your father?'

'Ask your father what?' said the booming voice. The hairy brute had crept up on them. Pnina trembled a little but said as bravely as she could:

'Good afternoon! I've come to ask permission to visit the rabbits. My sister wants to so much that she's become feverish, from so much wanting!'

'Good heavens!' said the hairy monster. 'What

have you said to this young lady, David?'

'I've said they c–c–could c–c–come and p–p–p–play with the rabbits.'

'Well,' said the hairy monster. 'I suppose there's no reason why they shouldn't.'

'We can talk to David as well,' said Pnina, 'and David can come to our house and be our friend. I have a brother called Eli who would like a new friend, I know. Maybe David could come home with me now.'

The hairy monster said: 'Just to accompany you then, as it's getting a little late – but be sure to come straight back, David.'

'My mother will never let him go home without giving him food,' Pnina said. 'Nobody comes into our house and leaves without eating.'

'That's very kind of you,' said the hairy monster. 'I will look forward to seeing you and your sister again when you come to visit the rabbits.'

'Thank you, sir. My sister will be so happy.'

David and Pnina walked in a friendly sort of silence for most of the way to the Genzels' house, then Pnina said:

'That's where I live . . . come on!'

David hesitated.

'I d–d–don't know if I sh–sh–should . . .' he began.

'Nonsense!' said Pnina, taking hold of his hand as though he were Miriam. 'Everyone will be so pleased to meet you. For my little sister, you're already a hero, because you are the owner of Snowy and Spotty.'

David laughed. 'S–S–Snowy and Sp–Sp–Spotty!'

he exclaimed. 'What funny names! Their real names are Benny and Ezra.'

'Don't tell Miriam,' said Pnina. 'She thinks Snowy and Spotty are wonderful names. Come and meet my brothers. Come and meet Eli.'

David climbed the stairs behind Pnina. She burst into the house, shouting: 'Miriam! Miriam! Look who's here! It's David, the owner of the rabbits.' Then she ran into the bedroom to tell her sister the whole story. Zehava came to see what all the noise was all about.

'Hello,' she said to David. 'How nice to see you. You must be a friend of Pnina's. Come and sit down and eat a piece of apple cake. Eli, come and meet this new friend.' Eli came to the table.

'I'm Eli,' he said smiling. 'What's your name?'

'D–D–D–David.'

'Well, hurry up and finish your cake and I'll show you my special climbing tree.'

David smiled and began to eat.

'Leave the poor boy alone,' said Zehava. 'Let him eat without choking. There'll be plenty of time for trees.'

Pnina came into the room.

'David,' she said. 'Miriam's better. She's really better. And she wants to meet the boy who owns the rabbits.'

'Will you go and tell her to wait?' said Zehava. 'The poor child can't even finish a bit of cake in peace. Tell her he's coming in a minute.'

'And after that,' said Eli, 'after you've visited Madame Miriam, then I'll show you my tree.'

David nodded happily and took another spoonful of cake.

BEYOND THE CROSS-STITCH
MOUNTAINS 1948

'I know! I've guessed!' said Harry. 'David married Miriam and then they came to the States to be my grandparents.'

Aunt Rachel laughed. 'I've never heard it put quite like that before. They went to America, as a lot of people have done over the years, to seek their fortune, but naturally their greatest ambition was to have you as a grandchild.'

'But Eli stayed behind, even though he was David's friend?'

'Yes, he did. He was my favourite uncle. Our family tree is complicated, isn't it? Look at this picture, for instance. This is Eli's daughter, Hadassah, who was always called Daskeh. I haven't seen this photograph for years. Daskeh has hardly changed.'

'I know her,' said Harry. 'I've been to her house in Haifa. It's up on a hill.'

'Mount Carmel,' said Aunt Rachel. 'Daskeh was always brave. I shall tell you a story about her. It happened at a time when Jerusalem was under siege.'

'What's that?' asked Harry.

'Surrounded on all sides by enemies, so that no

food could get into the city from the countryside. Oh, I remember it as if it were yesterday. We were all so hungry.'

'I'm hungry right now,' said Harry, thinking of a cake he knew was in the tin in the kitchen cupboard.

'Not in the way we were then. Listen.'

FRIDAY AFTERNOON

Hadassah (always called Daskeh) was wiping the clean counter even cleaner with a damp cloth. Soon, the grocery shop, like a small, dark cave hollowed into the wall of yellow stone, would close for the Sabbath. Daskeh's father, Eli Genzel, was in the back room, sitting at a small table and poking with a spoon at the slice of lemon in his tea.

'This lemon will have to go,' he muttered. 'How many cups can the poor thing float in without falling to bits? No flesh left, only brown rind.'

Daskeh answered from the shop: 'And you're lucky to have that, as you always say to me.' She put the cloth away, and came to sit with her father at the table.

'Are you ready to close, child?' he said.

'Close, open, what's the difference? There's so little to sell, these days. Except smells. I can't scrub

Historical note
During the spring of 1948, the Jewish part of the city of Jerusalem was besieged by the armies of the Arab nations. Food and water were very scarce, and both were rationed.

them out. Pickled herring, brown bread, soap – all the smells hanging around the shop like ghosts. They won't go away.'

'They are to remind us of happier days, perhaps . . .'

'Perhaps. But they make me feel sad. The cheese went this morning. Five hundred grams. I must have cut slices for the whole street. I'll be the best slicer of cheese in the whole of Jerusalem, soon. Transparent bits of cheese, I make. Nothing in them, hardly.' Daskeh poured some pale liquid from the teapot into a glass.

Eli ran his thumb along the wrinkles in his brow and said: 'Transparent cheese is cheese. No cheese is no cheese.'

'Transparent cheese is just as bad as no cheese, when you refuse to take money for it.'

'We must share, these days. And besides, there is so little to buy, what do we need money for?'

Daskeh was silent. She was drinking her tea and thinking of sugar. She thought about putting four cubes into her glass, remembering the way they lost their shape and crumbled into the liquid, and were whirled around by her spoon like tiny grains of diamond. She said: 'When this is all over, I shall put six cubes of sugar into every cup of tea.'

'Then it will be too sweet,' Eli smiled.

'Then I'll pour it down the sink, and make another cup. As many cups as I like. As strong as I like. All day long.'

'Isn't it time you went home to help your aunt prepare the Sabbath meal, such as it is? Go, child,

I'll close up the shop.'

Daskeh stood up and kissed her father. He said: 'Enjoy yourself, Daskele. You're a good girl, like your mother. You remind me of her, sometimes.'

Daskeh thought of the framed photograph of her mother that hung above the dark sideboard in the flat. She was, to the girl, a pretty stranger in a lace blouse buttoned up to the chin. A woman with a heavy coil of black hair arranged in a knot at the nape of her neck, and solemn, light eyes.

'I wish I had known her. I wish I could be pretty, like her.'

'To me, you are beautiful.' Eli kissed his daughter. 'And she, where she is, in heaven, is proud of you. Proud that at eleven years old you look after me, and work in the shop, and help your aunt at home.' Tears began to film Eli's eyes.

Daskeh said quickly: 'I must go now, Father. Take care of yourself until tonight.'

'Go in peace, child,' said Eli.

Daskeh walked through the shop and into the street. The light, striking sparks from the yellow stones all around her, dazzled her eyes. It was springtime already. Soon, on the almond tree in the courtyard of the house across the street, there would be blossoms. Daskeh walked up the hill along winding pavements of smooth, flat stones. From somewhere in the distance came the sound of the guns, but Daskeh hardly heard them. She was thinking how many thousands of times she must have followed this same way home, through streets with high walls close together, full of secret places, and unexpected gardens behind half-open wooden doors. Somewhere, beyond the flat, was the Jaffa Road. Somewhere, there were shops, cafés and cinemas to which she never went.

My life is always the same, she thought, the shop and the flat, the flat and the shop. Nothing different ever happens. I see only family and customers. I have some pretty dresses, but who wears pretty dresses to wrap up sugar rations? I wish I could have stayed at school. I wish Father could afford to pay someone to work in the shop instead of me. Danny is my only friend, really. He's funny, like a little animal, quiet, with furry, soft hair. He's only ten, and he knits in the shelter at night, even though he's a boy. The sound of the guns and the shells frightens him. He's nice.

Daskeh walked on. Silent, pale men with long sidelocks of hair, wearing black frock-coats and fur hats, passed her on their way to the synagogue. Small children were playing on the pavement, playing with stones or old pine cones left over from last year. Once upon a time, walking down this street on a Friday afternoon, you could smell the food cooking, all ready for the Sabbath. Once upon a time, this was the best part of the week, preparing for the day of rest. Daskeh made a list in her head of what she would have liked to make this afternoon, if there were no siege, and all the food in the world to eat. An apple strudel. Aunt Pnina could roll the dough, thought Daskeh, and I would slice apples into half-moon shapes, and chop the nuts and sprinkle the sugar and cinnamon, and eat more raisins than went into the cake. Then we'd roll the whole lot up in the stretchy dough, Aunt Pnina at one end and me at the other, and put it into the oven to bake. I forgot the milk. I have to dip my fingers in the milk and stroke the top of the strudel, so that it comes out brown and shiny. And I have to make little slits in the dough for the air to come out. It's a long time since we baked.

Mincing for meatballs was good, too. Aunt Pnina used to sit down for a cup of tea, while Daskeh did it all by herself, turning the handle of the silvery mincer with one hand, and feeding things into its wide mouth with the other. She used to make different coloured worms squash out of the little holes and into the bowl. Orange carrot worms, and pearly onion worms, and pink, meaty worms. Bread went into the mincer, too, and parsley and garlic: white and green-spotted worms. Then Aunt Pnina (who always managed to finish her tea just as the last morsel squished its way out), added an egg and salt, and mixed all the different colours up with a wooden spoon. Then she rolled the mixture into little balls and fried them in the big, black frying-pan, and put them into a white dish, decorated with blue, long-legged birds.

Daskeh came out of her daydream, and waved to her aunt, who was standing on the balcony of the flat. Every day, she stood there and waited. Watching. A little afraid. Every day, Daskeh waved from the same place, and Aunt Pnina, relieved that the short walk was nearly over, happy that Daskeh was nearly safe home in the flat, waved back from the third floor.

The building had thick walls, and Daskeh shivered in the chilly, grey entrance-hall. At night this place, with numbered letter-boxes fixed to one wall, became the Shelter. All the families from all the flats gathered there with blankets and candles when the firing from the guns grew louder. Daskeh ran up the stairs.

'There you are, then!' Aunt Pnina was standing at the door. 'Come in, Daskele, and give me a big hug, and then we'll start work.'

Daskeh hugged her aunt, pleased at the comfortable shape of her, sniffing the clean apron that, like the shop, seemed haunted by food-smells from the past. Aunt Pnina's hair was tucked out of sight under a blue scarf, and the skin around her eyes became creased when she smiled. 'Every wrinkle a sorrow, Daskele,' she used to say. 'But you're not even old,' Daskeh would answer. They went in together.

Everything that Daskeh loved was here. The tin in the wardrobe, rattling with thousands of jewel-slippery buttons, the shawls to dress up in, and the white cupboard full of Aunt Pnina's shoes. Aunt Pnina was vain about her tiny feet. 'Aristocratic feet,' she called them. 'Like a duchess.' There were thirty pairs of shoes in the white cupboard, and Daskeh fitted them now, but when she was very small, three or four years old, she had clomped for hours around the tiled floors, pretending to be a lady.

The best part of the flat was the balcony. You

could sit there on a Friday evening, with all the work done, and look at the domes and towers and roofs of the grey and golden city spread around, and watch for the first stars to appear in the turquoise sky, and mark the end of the Sabbath. On this balcony, there were cactus plants in squat, red pots. In the days when you could buy cucumbers in the market, Aunt Pnina used to pickle them in salty water and leave them in the sun in tall, glass jars, where they floated in the milky, pale-green liquid like dead things. But how sharp and salty and good they tasted with potato pancakes, or hard-boiled eggs, or chopped liver – with almost anything. The floor of the balcony was made of square, honey-coloured tiles. Each square had the shape of a flower cut into it. The tiles were unglazed, and caught and held the sunlight and the warmth. In the summer, in very hot weather, they were still warm to touch long after darkness had fallen.

'We'll lay the table first,' said Aunt Pnina, 'and

then go and see what's in the kitchen to eat.'

Daskeh folded the oilcloth (patterned with red flowers and all the way from America) and put it away in a drawer of the sideboard. Aunt Pnina brought the Sabbath cloth from the cupboard in the bedroom. It was made of white linen, with white embroidery all around the edge. They spread it over the table.

Daskeh put the glasses on the table, and said: 'There, it's finished, Aunt Pnina.'

'Good girl. Now come. Siege or no siege, the Sabbath will soon be here. We'll see what we can find to put in the old tin can.'

They went into the kitchen. The tin can, which, many years ago had held a few gallons of kerosene, was balanced on top of a primus stove. Before the siege, all the Sabbath food used to be packed into the tin can with great care, and wedged firmly with teatowels. Then, a small flame was lit on the primus stove, and the food would keep warm all through

Friday night and Saturday, when cooking was forbidden. The coffee and tea in bottles were lukewarm by Saturday morning, the whites of the hard-boiled eggs were baked to a pale brown, and the yolks had faded to the colour of moonlight.

'I wonder how long it will be before we have brown eggs again,' said Daskeh.

'If an egg came to me covered in polka dots, I would rejoice and sing,' said Aunt Pnina. 'But instead of eggs tonight, I have a special treat. A tin of sardines. And I will make some kind of pancake, though how it will taste without eggs, I don't know . . .'

'I'll open the tin,' Daskeh said, 'and I won't spill a drop of the oil.'

FRIDAY NIGHT

Outside the circle of candlelight, there was nothing but darkness and the rattle of the guns. The shelter was crowded. Daskeh sat next to Danny on the step and watched the faces, changed by the yellow light into masks full of black shadows that grew and shrank as the flames trembled. Mrs Sirkis from the second floor was moaning again.

'Listen to them,' she said, 'just listen. It's coming from the direction of Barclay's Bank tonight, I can tell. That's where the fighting is now. They're shelling the Bank. And my poor diamonds, locked up there, what will become of them? My lovely diamonds . . .'

'Madam,' said Grandfather Gluck, 'if you give

the diamonds to me, put them in my name, it would be the greatest pleasure in the world for me to worry about them. Nothing I'd like better.'

Mrs Sirkis promptly forgot her anguish and snapped: 'You, Mr Gluck, have no respect for property!'

'Because, madam, I have no property to respect. Your diamonds would be very good for me altogether.'

Mrs Sirkis sucked her teeth loudly, and folded her lips over them. There was nothing more to say.

Danny was knitting, frowning at the needles, shutting out of his ears every noise but their peaceful clicking. From time to time, an armoured lorry thundered by on the road outside, past the stone wall which blocked off the entrance to the flats. Big, square monsters, these armoured cars, with lamps for eyes. The lamps made rapid tracks of light along the walls as the lorries drove by, and Danny stopped knitting, holding himself stiffly until they had gone.

'What's that, Danny,' asked Daskeh, 'that you're making now? It's very pretty.'

'A scarf for winter.'

'You made a scarf before.'

Silence. Then: 'I only know how to make scarves.'

'I think you're very clever to be able to make anything. I've tried. My fingers turn into wooden clothes pegs. Aunt Pnina is desperate. Maybe if I watch you . . .'

'I have to go slowly. There's not so much wool left.'

'I can give you some. We unpicked a shawl the

other day. Aunt Pnina thought the colours would encourage me.'

'Did they?'

'No. I felt like crying. It was as if she were unpicking a rainbow. Anyway, if I give you the wool, you could knit it up again, couldn't you?'

'Thanks, Daskeh.' The tapping of his needles was lost in a long and very close-sounding burst of gunfire. 'That was very near us, wasn't it?'

'Are you frightened?'

'No. Yes. Yes, I am. Aren't you?'

'Yes, a little. But we're safe here, you know. The walls are thick. And we're all together.'

'It's not only us . . .' said Danny.

'Who then . . .?'

'Them. The others. Everyone who's fighting, on both sides. In danger.'

'Don't think of it now, Danny. Look, look at all the others, playing chess, reading books, some even sleeping. Listen, let me tell you what we had tonight. You'll never guess.'

'What?'

'Sardines. A whole tin. One sardine each, and the last one divided into three. It's very difficult to cut a sardine into three bits the same size. Where the tail is, it gets narrow, so you have to have a longer piece there, and a short piece up at the top where the fish is quite fat. My father spent ages carving it up and spooning out all the oil. It was heavenly. I licked the plate. I really did. Every drop.'

'We ate our last tin last week,' said Danny, 'but I still remember how it tasted.'

A voice whispered from the darkness: 'Children, come. Come. I have something for you. Something good. Daskeh, Danny, come to me.'

Daskeh hesitated. She knew who it was. Mrs Birnbaum from the first floor. Dirty clothes, and fingers like the claws of an ancient bird. Mrs Birnbaum, who watched the street all day from her balcony and talked to herself. Daskeh was a little afraid of her.

'Let's go, Danny. She can't hurt us. My father is here, and your mother. What can she do? Anyway, she might really have something good for us.'

The children stood up and stepped over bodies and stretched-out legs until they came to the darkest corner of the shelter. Mrs Birnbaum's eyes glittered in the candlelight. She put out a claw, and took Daskeh's hand.

'Take, girl, take. It's for you. What do I need it for?'

'Thank you, Mrs Birnbaum,' said Daskeh. Danny said nothing. Daskeh could feel something hard, wrapped in paper, against her palm, as the claw held her hand imprisoned.

'Enjoy them in good health,' said the old woman. 'Sieges are for crones like me, and not for growing children, isn't that so?'

'Yes,' said Danny 'and thank you very much.'

Back in their place on the step, Daskeh opened the bit of crumpled paper.

'Aniseed balls!' she breathed. 'How beautiful! How marvellous! Four. Two each. Oh, lovely! Here's your share.'

'Maybe we should each have one now, and keep

one for tomorrow?' said Danny.

'Are you mad? What for? Ooh, I'm going to suck and suck them very gently. They'll last for ages. Maybe all night.' Daskeh put one into her mouth, and closed her eyes.

'They change colour,' said Danny after a while, and Daskeh took her sweet out to have a look at it. It had been brown, and was now orange. It turned purple, pink and green and when all the colours were gone, only a tiny white ball the size of a pea was left. Danny sucked his to the end, but Daskeh grew impatient, and crunched the pale, sugary heart to powder with her teeth. Then she sighed happily and began to suck the second aniseed ball.

Daskeh leaned against the wall with a cushion under her head, and sucked at her sweet until she fell asleep.

Much later, the silence woke her, and the cold. The candles were out, and in the metal-grey light that filled the shelter, she could see the lumps of bodies bunched under blankets, and hear the muffled snores of old men. No more guns. Beside her, Danny lay curled up like a cat, clutching his scarf. Daskeh shook him, whispered in his ear: 'Danny. Wake up, Danny. They're all asleep. It's morning. Wake up.' Danny opened his eyes, awake at once.

'It's all right,' said Daskeh gently. 'It's daytime. No guns, no lorries. Let's go up on the roof.'

'We're not allowed to . . .'

'But everyone is asleep. They'll never know. We won't stay long. Listen to the snoring! Just be careful not to tread on anybody.'

Danny still looked worried, but he followed Daskeh out of the shelter and up and up and up on to the flat roof of the building.

'Why do we come here?' he asked. 'There's nothing but boring old water tanks and stupid lines of washing.'

'I like it. You can see quite far. Over there, there's the King David Hotel and the Y.M.C.A. tower and the hills, and all the streets I've hardly ever been in, the streets I don't know.'

'Where's Rehavia? Which way?'

'There, I think.' Daskeh pointed towards the horizon. 'It's very grand, that part of town. They have trees in the streets, with railings round them. I went there once.'

'It's cold here,' said Danny. 'Can't we go back?'

'Don't be such a baby.'

The sky was the colour of pearls, the colour of doves, and the walls of the city were pale in the dawn, like good butter. Daskeh said: 'I feel as if I could walk for miles and never come back. I feel as if I could fly away, miles away, away from the shop, and this building, away to some strange place that no one has ever been to . . .'

'That's silly,' said Danny. 'There are no strange places out there. Only the rest of Jerusalem.'

'Shut up. What do you know about it? I'm just bored, that's all. I want to see something different. What's silly about that?'

'Nothing, I suppose.'

'You suppose . . . What do you want, then? Just

to stay here knitting every day? Don't you ever want to go somewhere else?'

Danny sat down on an upturned tin tub. 'There's somewhere I want to go to.'

'Where?'

'There. In Rehavia.'

'What's there?'

'It's where my mother's aunt lives. Aunt Simha, she's called.'

'Then why don't you go, if she's family? Why don't you go with your parents?'

'They don't visit her any more,' said Danny. 'They had a quarrel. Something stupid . . .'

'Is she nice, this aunt of yours?'

'She's funny. Strange. She used to give me cakes made out of sesame seeds, all stuck together. They were diamond-shaped.'

'Well, you won't get those now. No sugar, so no cakes.'

'She's fat. She wears about twenty gold bracelets on each arm. She hasn't got very much hair.'

'Could you find the way?'

'I don't know. I've never tried.'

'Well, do you know the name of the street?'

'Yes,' said Danny. 'Ussishkin Street. And I know the number, 22.'

'Then we could ask.'

'Yes, we could. Do you want to come?'

'They wouldn't let us go alone,' said Daskeh, 'and your parents have quarrelled.'

Danny smiled. 'We don't have to tell them. We could just go . . .'

Daskeh felt a fluttering in her stomach, like a bird. Fear and pleasure mixed together. They would run away, no one would know where they were . . .

'We'd have to arrange it very carefully.' Daskeh sat down next to Danny on the tub, and began to organize. 'Listen. Everyone must think we're with someone else. I'll tell my father I can't help in the shop because I have to help Aunt Pnina with something or other. Aunt Pnina will think I'm in the shop till five o'clock. Your mother goes out and gets her rations very early in the morning, so you can tell her I've asked you to keep me company behind the counter. She'll never know. No one will know. If we leave early enough, we'll be back long before it's dark.'

'What a good plan. You are clever, Daskeh. I'd never have thought of all that. It'll be an adventure, won't it? When will we go?'

'Tuesday, I think. We'll talk about it again, don't worry. Come on, though, now. We must go down to the shelter. They'll be waking up soon.'

They tiptoed down the stairs.

'See,' said Daskeh. 'What did I tell you? They're all still asleep.'

TUESDAY

'Eat it, Daskele. What are you staring at it for?' Aunt Pnina pointed to the teaspoonful of jam lying on the saucer. 'It's full of sugar. To give you strength for the day.'

Daskeh hardly heard her. Absent-mindedly, she

picked up the spoon, and licked the red stickiness very delicately with her tongue. Then she took a mouthful of water. If you managed it right, you could make the jam last until every drop of the water had gone.

'You're not with us today at all. Dreaming. It's not like you,' said Aunt Pnina.

Daskeh looked across to the other end of the table. On the wall behind her aunt's head, she could see the coloured zigzags of the cross-stitched wall-hanging, like mountains from a country visited in dreams: orange, scarlet, brown and royal blue peaks and valleys, green and yellow foothills at the bottom. This hanging, the size of a blanket, had always been there on the wall, and Daskeh had grown so used to it, she scarcely saw it any more. But now, on this day, to prevent Aunt Pnina from noticing how excited she was, she said: 'I was thinking about the cross-stitch mountains. Did you really make it? All by yourself?'

'How many times have I told you? A hundred? A thousand?'

'But tell it again. How old were you?'

'Seventeen. And beautiful. You wouldn't believe. With an eighteen inch waist. Well, twenty inches, maybe. Look at me now. Many more inches round the waist, eh?' Aunt Pnina patted her stomach. 'Well, my mother had arranged for me to marry a young man. He was from a good family. A religious family. But his parents had trouble persuading him to come and meet me. He was in love with someone else.'

'Did he come in the end?'

'Yes, he came. And it was like Romeo and Juliet. One look at me, and that was that. The other girl was forgotten. The wedding was all arranged. I began to embroider that as a bedspread.'

'Then what happened?'

'You see how the colours start bright and happy? Look, yellow and red and orange, and green, can you see?'

'Yes,' said Daskeh.

'And have you seen this?' Aunt Pnina pointed to a band of black somewhere near the middle.

'That was when he died, wasn't it?'

'That's right. Poor Avram. Twenty years old. He looked so healthy, too. A most terrible fever took him. After I had finished the black bit, I left the blanket in the chest. I left it there for two years. Then when Sarah was to be married, I took it out. I thought I'd finish it for her, and I did, but when the time came to give it to her, I couldn't part with it, so I put it up here. And here it still is. Maybe for you, when you are married. I'm an old woman now. What do I need it for? Haven't we got enough problems without being sad about what's finished? You, you're like my own daughter, so you shall have it.'

'How lovely, Aunt Pnina. Thank you. I haven't looked at it properly for such a long time. It's beautiful. Like mountains, and blue sky right at the top.'

'Come now, Daskele, it's time you went to the shop. Your father will be waiting.'

'Yes,' said Daskeh, and kissed her aunt goodbye.

'I'll be back this evening. Have a good day, darling Aunt Pnina. I love you so much.'

'What's this? What's this? All this love, so early in the morning! You are funny today, girl. I don't know what's the matter with you. Get along, now, or you'll be late.'

Daskeh ran down the stairs, and knocked on Danny's door. His mother opened it.

'Hello, Mrs Rakov. Is Danny ready?'

'Yes, he's ready. Is it all right with your father that he should be in the shop all day? I meant to ask your father last night, but what with one thing and another . . .'

'Yes, it's fine,' said Daskeh, smiling at Mrs Rakov in her relief. What a narrow escape. If Mrs Rakov had asked Eli . . . Daskeh didn't like to think about it. 'It'll be company for me.'

Danny was standing behind his mother. He looked worried.

'Come, Danny. Daskeh's waiting.' Mrs Rakov put a paper bag into his hand. 'Here's something for your lunch. Mr Genzel has enough worries without having to feed you.'

'What is it?' asked Danny.

'Nothing much. A couple of matzos, that's all, and a bit of cheese.'

Daskeh smiled again, pleased at how well everything was turning out. Here was a picnic lunch provided for them. Yesterday, she had saved a biscuit, and it lay now wrapped in paper, deep in the pocket of her brown cotton skirt. A feast.

'Goodbye, Mother,' said Danny.

'Goodbye, Danny, be good. Don't be a trouble for Mr Genzel.'

'I won't, Mother,' said Danny, and waved to her as he followed Daskeh down the stairs.

Outside, in the street, Daskeh said: 'Let's see if all the balconies are clear. We don't want anyone to see us going the wrong way. Is Mrs Birnbaum there?' They looked. Every balcony was empty.

'Right,' said Daskeh. 'Now run, and don't stop till we get to the hospital.'

She started off down the hill, with Danny running behind her. They came, panting, to a low wall with railings on top of it, and leaned against it to rest.

'Let's cross to the other side of the road,' said Danny.

'Why? What's wrong with this side?'

'I don't like all the sick people on the pavement in their dressing-gowns.'

'Those are the ones that aren't sick, silly. The sick ones are in bed. These are the ones who are getting better, and need fresh air. They haven't got a garden, so they sit outside on the pavement sometimes, that's all.'

'Please let's cross. They look sick and yellow and old. Please.'

Daskeh sighed. 'All right, I suppose so,' she said, and she took Danny's hand as they crossed the road and continued down the hill.

They passed queues of people with buckets in their hands, lining up for their ration of water. Long, tight curls of barbed wire lay in the road and there were soldiers with angry-looking rifles slung over their shoulders. Nobody took any notice of the thin girl in the brown skirt and black stockings and the boy almost running to keep up with her. Then the children stopped to look into the window of a jeweller's shop. The jeweller saw them for a moment from behind his counter, and a thought like a leaf blown by the wind flew into his head: 'What are those children doing, alone, here in the middle of town, in the middle of a war?' But just then, his wife screeched for something from upstairs, and the man left his counter to see what she wanted. By the time he came back, the children had gone. He worried about them from time to time for the rest of the morning.

'My feet are hurting.'

'Come on, Danny, you can't stop there. Look, it's not much further. This *is* the street, isn't it?'

'Yes. That's the house there. With the pointed trees in the garden, and the blue flowers hanging over the wall.'

'Then what are we waiting for?'

'I don't know.' Danny looked down to where the toe of his shoe was scratching patterns in the dust. 'Maybe she's out. Maybe she won't want to see us. Maybe we shouldn't have come . . .'

'It's a fine time you've chosen, haven't you, to say all this? Now that we're practically sitting on her doorstep? Why didn't you think of it before? This was all your idea.'

Danny's eyes filled with tears. 'Don't be cross, Daskeh. I just . . . I don't know, I feel nervous.'

'Well, stop feeling nervous this minute. And stop snivelling. You're nothing but a crybaby.'

'Don't be angry, Daskeh. Make friends. Please.'

'I *am* friends,' shouted Daskeh, 'but you're such a ninny. Here. Take my hanky and blow your nose.' Danny rubbed his nose obediently. 'Now. Stand up straight, and put a smile on that face, for once. We're going visiting. Follow me.' Daskeh strode off towards the gate. Danny walked beside her, dragging his feet. As they stood in front of the door, Daskeh suddenly felt nervous herself. She looked at Danny's white face, and nearly, so nearly took him by the hand, and ran away. You're not much braver than he is, Hadassah Genzel, she told herself. Ring that bell. And she put her finger on it before she could change her mind.

The door was opened by an enormously fat woman. Daskeh saw the gold bracelets on her arms, just as Danny had said. This was Aunt Simha. Nobody said anything for a while. Aunt Simha looked at Daskeh, then at Danny, then at Daskeh again. Danny said: 'Don't you recognize me, Aunt Simha? It's Danny Rakov.'

The old woman clapped her hand over her mouth and stared. Then she shouted: 'Danny, my darling! Such a long time ... What a big boy. How you've grown!' and she almost buried the boy in the flapping shawls and fringes and trailing pieces of lace in which she was draped. Danny struggled for air after a few moments, and his aunt released him.

'This is my friend, Daskeh. She ...'

'Don't stand here, children. Daskeh. So good to

see a friend of Danny's. Come into the house. Come and sit. Have you walked?'

'We walked all the way,' said Daskeh, but Aunt Simha was no longer listening. Like a fat butterfly, she had settled on another topic of conversation.

'Are you hungry? You must be hungry. Children are always hungry, isn't that right? Let me see now, what do I have for you? Not much, these days, but sit, and I will bring.'

Daskeh and Danny sat on a plush-covered sofa. The shutters were closed, and bars of sunlight striped the carpet. Aunt Simha was making clattering noises in the kitchen.

'Is your aunt very rich?' whispered Daskeh.

'Yes, I think so,' said Danny. 'I think she's a bit of a miser. That's what my mother says. She wouldn't give them money to buy a shop, or something like that. How did you know she was rich?'

'The carpet is all red and silky. And look at the shiny copper things all over the place. And velvet curtains. They look a little dusty, but aren't they grand? It's like something in a book.'

Aunt Simha waddled back into the room, carrying a brass tray.

'Danny,' she said, 'be a good boy and put that little table in front of the sofa. See what your aunty has found for you, my love.'

The table was inlaid with a mosaic of mother-of-pearl.

'It's beautiful,' said Daskeh.

'Beautiful things I have,' said Aunt Simha sadly, 'only happiness I lack. But today, such a wonderful surprise, to see my darling Danny again. Eat now, children. See, I have some sesame seed cakes.'

Daskeh closed her eyes. It's a dream, she thought. In a moment I shall wake up and find myself spooning tea into little pieces of newspaper in my father's shop. When she opened her eyes, the diamond-shaped biscuits were still there.

'Take, Daskeh. Don't be shy,' said Aunt Simha. The two children began to eat and went on eating until the gaps between their teeth were full of tiny seeds, and their mouths sweet with the taste of them. Aunt Simha nodded from her chair, her chins wobbling with pleasure. She said: 'Now you will have tea. With mint leaves. And sugar.' She went into the kitchen again.

'How wonderful that was!' said Daskeh, chasing the last few crumbs around the plate with a sticky finger. 'And tea with sugar ... What about the mint? Will she mind if I don't have mint?'

'It's what they drink in Morocco. That's where she was born. Mint tea tastes lovely.'

'I think I'd rather have lemon, but I suppose it would be rude to ask, after she's been so nice.'

'Aren't you glad I thought of coming?' said Danny.

Daskeh laughed. 'Danny Rakov! You wanted to go back. Remember? It's thanks to me we're here at all.'

The mint tea was delicious. I must tell Aunt Pnina about it, thought Daskeh and for a moment felt a longing to be at home with her aunt. What would she be doing? What would she say if she ever found out about this visit? Daskeh shivered, and looked up at the clock. Whatever happened, they must not arrive home late. Aunt Pnina was probably sponging the black and yellow tiled floors, or maybe ironing . . . Her father was in the shop, dealing alone with all the customers pleading, wheedling, sure that Genzel was keeping some morsel of food from them. They used to pry into the back room to see what treasures were hidden there. Her father wouldn't know how to manage. Daskeh chuckled to herself as she remembered the look on Mrs Meltzer's face . . . I certainly lost my temper with her . . . dragged her behind the counter and opened every drawer to show her it was empty, then banged it shut! And I yelled at her, too. It's a good thing Father was out of the shop. He would have made me take some of our rations over to her house. I would have had to apologize . . .

Aunt Simha talked incessantly. About the siege, about the old days, about her youth, about how sickly Danny had been as a baby. Pointed silver hands made their way round the clock, and the bars of light lengthened across the carpet.

'Aunt Simha,' said Danny, after Daskeh had kicked him on the shin and pointed at the clock, 'we have to go home now.'

'So soon? You only just came. Why do you have to go so soon? What's the hurry?'

'It's been really lovely,' said Daskeh. 'We have enjoyed it. And thank you for the tea and the beautiful sesame cakes. We have to be home before five o'clock, and it's quite a long way.'

'But your mother won't worry, Danny, if she knows you're with me,' said Aunt Simha.

'No,' said Danny quickly, 'but we must go. Daskeh has to help her aunt prepare the supper.'

'Well, you will come again soon. Both of you. Won't you? Please?'

Aunt Simha looked so sad that the children said 'Yes.'

'Good,' said Aunt Simha, and struggled out of her chair. 'Now, I'm going to give you both something to take home. A present. Come with me. I have it in the kitchen.'

On the table, lying in a saucer, were two eggs. Real eggs. Aunt Simha picked them up, and wrapped them in a clean cloth.

'Take care of them, now. Don't break them.'

'Are you sure, Aunty?' said Danny. 'Don't you need them?'

'Do I look as if I need food?' Aunt Simha laughed. 'You need it more. Have one each. Have it for supper. And think of me when you eat it, and remember to come again.'

Daskeh took the eggs, and held them gently in her hands. Aunt Simha covered her for a moment in waves of material as she kissed her goodbye. Then Danny disappeared for a long time under the draperies. Aunt Simha watched the children going down the road until they turned the corner. Then she started crying quietly, dabbing her eyes with a stray corner of lace. From far away came the sound of the guns.

'I'll have mine boiled,' said Daskeh. 'Soft boiled.'

'I think I'll have an omelette.'

'Or fried is nice,' said Daskeh, 'but it's a waste of oil. Boiled is best. My arms are hurting from carrying them so carefully. I feel as if I'm holding a baby.'

'Let me have them for a bit,' said Danny.

'You'd probably drop them.'

'I wouldn't.'

'You would.'

'Wouldn't.'

'All right. Here. Take them for a while. But if you drop them, I'll kill you. I will really.' Daskeh gave Danny the eggs. Then she bent down to take a stone out of her shoe. Danny walked on.

There was no one in the street. As Daskeh ran to catch up with Danny, he shouted out: 'Daskeh! What are you hitting me for? What have I done?' and dropped the eggs. They burst out of the cloth as they fell to the ground, and the yolks mingled with the yellow dust on the pavement. Daskeh couldn't even open her mouth to cry out. She stared at the smashed eggs, and felt a scream of rage rising in her throat. She could see nothing but the spreading pools of yolk and crushed fragments of shell. Then –

'Daskeh, I'm bleeding,' said Danny.

Daskeh looked at him. He held out his hand. It was streaked with blood, sticky with it. How? Why? What was that he had shouted out? Something about her hitting him. She hadn't touched him. All the warmth rushed out of her heart. She opened her mouth, and no sound came. Thudding noises filled her head. Danny had been shot. Had there been guns? Yes, there they were, still, tap-tapping in the distance. On the wall, just behind the children, there was a bullet-hole. A stray bullet, it must have been, to have come so far. A freak. Hurting poor Danny like that. At last, Daskeh said: 'Sit down, Danny. Let me see it. Where is it?'

'Here, on my shoulder.'

Daskeh tore Danny's shirt from round the wound, and looked. All the blood made her feel sick, but Danny, she could see, was biting his lip trying not to cry, and she knew that he would, if she looked at all worried.

'It's not so bad,' she said. 'Just a lot of blood. A graze from the bullet, that's all. Like the kind of cut you get from a bad fall. I'll clean it up. Can you help me to take your shirt off?'

Together they took off the shirt, and Daskeh mopped up the blood. Then she took her own handkerchief and tied it as well as she could round Danny's shoulder, over the wound.

'There, now. We'll hurry to get home. I suppose we're going to have to tell them everything. There's no hiding something like this.' Daskeh felt angry with Danny for a moment for spoiling the smooth working of her plan, and being stupid enough to stand in the way of a stray bullet, and drop the eggs. Just then, as if he had had the same thought, Danny started crying. Howling and sobbing and weeping for his mother. Daskeh forgot her anger, and sat down beside him on the pavement, and held his head against her shoulder.

'Don't cry, Danny. Be brave. I know it hurts. But we'll soon be home. I'll help you. Don't worry. You'll be with your mother very soon.'

'But the eggs . . . I dropped the eggs. You said you'd kill me if I dropped them. You were going to have a boiled egg tonight.'

'Never mind about me killing you and boiled eggs,' said Daskeh, suddenly aware of how near Danny's shoulder was to his head, how nearly he had escaped. 'Stand up now, if you can.'

'I don't think I can, really.' Danny spoke snuffily, through his tears.

'It's lucky you're a titch, then, isn't it, if I'm going to have to carry you all the way . . . and lucky you had the sense not to get shot at in Rehavia.'

Daskeh lifted the boy onto her hip, as she had seen mothers do with small children. He was not as heavy as a big box of groceries, but she had never had to carry a box of groceries so far. Danny was still crying, but more quietly now.

'Do you know the song?' said Daskeh.

'Which song?'

She began to sing:

> 'Mother said to Danny
> My boy is brave and good,
> My boy never cries
> Like a tiny baby.
>
> I never, ever cry
> And I'm not a tiny baby,
> But why, Mother, why
> Do the tears come all by themselves?'

Danny smiled and said: 'No, I've never heard that song before. It's funny, isn't it?'

'Yes,' said Daskeh 'and also quite sad.'

The children were silent as Daskeh struggled up the hill. Danny's shoulder had begun to bleed again. She could see the hospital now, with the old, yellow people on the pavement outside. Hospital. Daskeh nearly dropped Danny in her relief.

'Danny, I'm going to take you to hospital. They'll put something on your shoulder to make it better. Also, your mother and Aunt Pnina and my father won't be so angry. They'll see that we know what to do, how to take care of ourselves.'

'I'm not going in there,' shouted Danny. 'I'm frightened. I want my mother.'

'Well, you can't get to your mother without me, and I'm taking you to hospital first, so you can howl all you like.'

Daskeh pushed her way past the people lying about in the entrance, and dropped Danny onto the lap of a startled nurse in a white dress.

'He's been hit by a bullet,' she said. 'Could you have a look, please?'

The nurse hurried to fetch a doctor, and they began to carry Danny down the corridor. Daskeh followed them.

'There's really no need for you to come, dear,' said the nurse. 'He'll be out in a minute, as soon as we've dressed the wound.'

'I'm coming,' said Daskeh. 'I'm supposed to be looking after him. He'll be scared if I don't come.'

'Let her come,' said the doctor. 'It doesn't matter...'

Daskeh watched as they cleaned the wound and put some ointment on it, and a bandage.

The nurse talked to Daskeh as she worked.

'Where do you live?'

'Not far. 9, Chancellor Street. Just up the road.'

'We haven't got an ambulance at the moment, but if you wait, maybe we can get one to take you home.'

'Oh, no,' said Daskeh, 'thank you.' (Aunt Pnina, seeing an ambulance from the balcony, oh, never, never!) 'I'll carry him. He's very light.'

'Is he your brother?'

'He's my friend. He lives in the flat downstairs. We went to visit his aunt. We didn't tell anyone we were going, you see, so we don't want them to be frightened by an ambulance.'

'Yes, I see. Very well. There's nothing very wrong with his shoulder. You tied it up very nicely, young lady. It'll be better it two or three days, but tell his mother he should be in bed at least twenty-four hours.'

'Yes, I will. Thank you very much. Come on, Danny.' Daskeh picked him up, and walked out of the hospital.

Aunt Pnina just happened to be on the balcony and looking down the street, when she saw what was unmistakeably Daskeh coming towards the building from the wrong direction. Carrying Danny! Why weren't they coming from the shop? Why were they coming so early? Danny seemed to be asleep. Why wasn't he wearing a shirt? Something was very wrong indeed. Aunt Pnina asked herself no more questions. She ran to the front door of the flat, and down the stairs to the street. She was coming out of the entrance just as Daskeh reached it.

'Daskele, Danny, what's been happening? Why are you carrying him? Where's your father? Why aren't you in the shop?'

'Oh, Aunt Pnina, I'm so glad, so happy to see you. Danny was grazed by a bullet. We didn't go to the shop. We went to visit his aunt. We didn't want to tell you. Not his aunt, his mother's aunt . . .'

'Whose aunt doesn't matter. Why are we standing talking in the street with a hurt child? Come, I'll carry him now, and we'll take him up to his mother. How far have you carried him?'

'I don't know. Quite far.'

Aunt Pnina smiled and said nothing.

'I took him to the hospital down there, and they put a bandage on. He's to stay in bed for twenty-four hours.'

Outside Danny's flat, Aunt Pnina said to Daskeh: 'You go on up. I'll explain it all to Mrs Rakov. You've had enough trouble for one day. The door's open.'

Daskeh ran up the stairs to the third floor. She went into the empty flat and sat down. Home. She was home. She looked at the cross-stitch hanging on the wall, the lines of coloured mountains, the shapes of unknown lands and hidden valleys, and began to tremble, suddenly cold. When Aunt Pnina came up from talking to Mrs Rakov, Daskeh took one look at her aunt and burst into tears.

'Oh, Aunt Pnina, what if something dreadful had happened to him?'

Aunt Pnina sat down next to Daskeh and put her arm gently round the girl's shoulders.

'Nothing dreadful happened. Just a graze. It could have been a fall. When your father was Danny's age, he broke his nose falling out of a tree. These things happen.'

'But we ran away . . . We never told anyone where we were going . . .'

'That's something else, Daskele. Why didn't you tell anyone? That was foolish. And dangerous.'

'Because you would have stopped us. You wouldn't have let us go alone. And I was so bored. So tired of the same thing every day, the same places, the same people, everything always the same. I never go anywhere different. I never see new places. I wanted . . . I don't know . . . I just wanted to run away for a little while. I'm sorry.'

'Sorry you don't have to be,' said Aunt Pnina. 'When I was young I was just the same. I remember, when I embroidered those mountains, imagining strange countries, oh, marvellous places beyond the rim of every hill. When I was young, and, if I'm honest, even now, sometimes, that was where I wanted to be – somewhere else.'

'Then you aren't angry with me?'

'It's too late for that. And you're in no fit state to be shouted at, and I'm so thankful to God that neither you nor Danny was badly hurt, that I feel like singing for joy. But instead of singing, I'll make tea and we will talk about all the places we will go to together. When the fighting is over. Full of bullet-holes, like a sieve, I'm not ready to be, even for you.'

Daskeh laughed. 'What did you tell Mrs Rakov?'

'Mrs Rakov? She wasn't in a mood to listen to me, poor thing. But she said, "Thank God Daskeh was there . . . what would have happened without her?" '

'He'd have been safe at home all the time, that's what,' said Daskeh. 'But on the other hand, he wouldn't have had those cakes.'

'What cakes?'

'Sesame seed cakes, we had. And tea with mint. And sugar. It was beautiful, Mrs Rakov's aunt is very rich and very fat.'

'Come and tell me, while I make the tea,' said Aunt Pnina, and Daskeh went with her aunt into the kitchen.

TUESDAY NIGHT

There was a mattress in the shelter for Danny. Daskeh was sitting on it, looking at Danny, leaning against the pillows.

'Does it hurt?' she wanted to know.

'Not badly, really. But I can't knit.'

'Never mind. I've got my wool all ready for you as soon as you want it. Was your mother angry?'

'No. I was surprised. She says she's going to take me to Aunt Simha's again, when I'm better. She says it's time the quarrel was made up. You can come too. Maybe we'll get some eggs again. I'm sorry about the eggs, Daskeh.'

'You're stupid. Who cares about the eggs? You should go to sleep now, or you won't get better quickly.'

'Sing me a song.'

'Which one?'

'Any song. A lullaby.'

Daskeh began to sing:

> *'Night, oh night*
> *the wind is blowing.*
> *Night, oh night*
> *Listen to the song.*
> *Night, oh night*
> *a star is singing.*
> *Sleep, oh sleep*
> *and blow the candle out.'*

By the time the lullaby was finished, Danny was asleep. Daskeh curled up at his feet, and closed her eyes. I'm so tired, she thought, I'll be asleep very soon. But she lay awake for a long time with her eyes shut, listening to the waves of voices murmuring in the corners of the shelter, listening to the pounding of the guns.

DREAMS OF FIRE 1950

'What happened to Danny?' Harry asked. 'Did he marry Daskeh?'

'Certainly not!' Aunt Rachel smiled. 'You can't expect everyone you meet in a story to turn up later as a relation.'

'But they stayed friends, didn't they?'

'Yes, they did. I'll tell you another story about them. Listen.'

*   *   *

One Wednesday afternoon in August, Danny lay on top of his bed and thought he knew exactly what it felt like to be a loaf of bread, baking on a hot shelf in the oven. The shutters had been closed to keep out the worst of the heat, but thin stripes of sunlight always managed to creep in, and those stripes now lay across Danny's bare legs. I look like a zebra, he thought, and in a minute I'll have to face Daskeh. It's nearly time for music.

Danny and Daskeh took piano lessons from Mrs Strauss, who lived in Rehavia, and on Wednesday afternoons they went to her apartment together. Danny had his lesson first and Daskeh waited for him, then she had her lesson and he waited for her and they came home together. It was a very satisfactory arrangement. He sighed. She'll be angry with me, he thought. She'll have to go all by herself, and she'll be annoyed with me. Tears prickled behind his eyes and he blinked them away. Everything was quite bad enough without adding tears to it. Tears would make everything worse. Someone knocked at the door, and Danny heard his mother opening it, and talking to Daskeh. What Daskeh said he couldn't hear, because she was still on the landing outside.

'Danny's not very well,' his mother was saying. 'I don't know exactly what . . . I can't find anything wrong, but he doesn't sleep. Sometimes I hear him walking about in the middle of the night. There's no getting two words out of him, well, you know how stubborn he can be . . . can't let him go to music today. I'm sure Mrs Strauss will understand. What? Really? Yes, I suppose so. If you've got the time. Come in for a moment. I'm sure he'll be happy to see you.'

Oh, no, thought Danny and turned away from the door of his room to face the wall. She's coming in. She's going to talk to me. She's going to ask me. I can't bear it. What will I tell her?

'Hello, Danny,' said Daskeh, who had come in and immediately sat down beside him on the bed. 'What's wrong with you? Why aren't you coming with me? We could have a doughnut at the Café Allenby.'

'Nothing's wrong.'

'Then why are you in bed?'

'I'm not in bed. It's too hot. I'm on the bed.'

Daskeh sighed. 'You know exactly what I mean. Are you sick?'

'Not really.'

'Have you got a headache?'

'No.'

'Stomach-ache?'

'No.'

'Ear-ache?'

Danny turned round, exasperated.

'Since when have you become a doctor? I'm *not* sick. I just . . .' He fell silent, and looked away.

'Just what?'

'I just haven't been sleeping very well.'

'I know. Your mother says she hears you walking around in the night. But why not?'

'I stop myself.'

'What?'

'I stop myself from sleeping. That's why I walk around.' Danny suddenly seemed absorbed in a tiny speck on his pillow.

'I'm fed up with this!' Daskeh stood up. 'Stop pretending that pillow's the most fascinating thing you've ever seen in your life and tell me why you're being so stupid. Tell me why you're making yourself ill on purpose. Tell me why you don't sleep. I've never heard of anyone doing anything like that before.'

Danny said: 'It's hard to explain. I don't want to sleep because I don't like the dreams I have when I do. Nightmares, that's what they are. I have night-mares every night about Bab-el-Waad.'

It was Daskeh's turn to be silent. Bab-el-Waad was a village in the hills outside Jerusalem. In the 1948 war, a convoy of trucks had been ambushed and set on fire there, and now the rusting metal skeletons of those trucks stood among the rocks and trees as a memorial to all who had died during the attack. There was even a song about it, which you could hear almost every time you turned on the wireless.

'Have you been to Bab-el-Waad?' Daskeh asked.

'I went with the Scouts, in the spring. And now I have nightmares all the time. One nightmare, really, because it's always the same. I'm in a truck, and it's standing on the side of the hill, and it starts burning. I can see flames creeping along the bonnet, towards me. I can feel the heat. I can see other vehicles on fire all around me, and people are walking about and they're on fire too. Oh, it's horrible, Daskeh. I can't describe to you how horrible. Can you imagine what it must have been like to be trapped in one of those trucks? I can't get it out of my mind. It makes me so frightened, Daskeh, that I'd rather just not sleep, but it's hard to keep awake sometimes. My eyes close up in the end all by themselves, and then the dreams start up all over again, as if they've been waiting on the insides of my eyelids, waiting for my eyes to close.'

'I don't know what to say, Danny,' said Daskeh. 'It's awful for you. Perhaps if you talk about it a lot, then the nightmares will go away. That's what my father says.'

'I can only tell you,' said Danny. 'Everyone at school would think I was a baby. They all think battles are wonderful, and soldiers are heroes who never get hurt. And everyone thinks we should be brave, us boys, just like grown-up soldiers. I'd never, ever tell any of them. Do you remember the victory parade through the streets when the war ended? How we stood on your balcony, shouting and cheering, and threw oranges down to the marching men? Do you remember how splendid the music sounded and how tall and strong all the soldiers looked? They looked as if they didn't know what fear was. I try to think about that, and not about Bab-el-Waad, and during the day it's easy.'

'Danny, I have to go to music now,' said Daskeh. 'I'll tell Mrs Strauss you've got a stomach-ache. And I'll come and visit you again.'

She waved to him from the door as she left the room.

Daskeh hurried to Rehavia, thinking about Danny. She had spoken to him for so long that there was no time to buy a doughnut. Perhaps his mother should get pills from the doctor to make him sleep. Should she tell Mrs Strauss the truth? No, stomach-ache sounded more reasonable, and besides, she'd promised Danny. Breathless from walking so quickly, Daskeh arrived at her piano teacher's building just as another pupil was leaving. Mrs Strauss met her in the hall.

'And where is little Danny today?' she asked. Daskeh smiled, thinking how Danny would have hated to be called 'little'.

'He's not very well,' she said. 'He has stomach-ache and sends you his apologies.'

'In that case, we have some extra time. Come into the salon and have a drink. My son Alex is there . . . you remember me telling you about him. It's so hot. I'm sure you need some refreshment.' She bustled into the apartment, and Daskeh followed her.

She always felt enormous in Mrs Strauss's apartment. It was full of tiny china ornaments in pale pastel colours balanced on shaky little wooden tables. The rugs were pale too, and all the furniture looked daintier and more flimsy than furniture is supposed to look, so that Daskeh never sat down on a chair without fearing that it would break. Mrs Strauss (who was tiny and doll-like too, to go with her house) wore mauve dresses and had a bun perched right on top of her head. She wore the same black laced-up shoes all the year round, and today Daskeh felt sweaty just thinking of them. Mrs Strauss had magic fingers. That was what she told Daskeh, and Daskeh saw no reason to disbelieve her. The magic fingers, when they were not racing up and down the keys of the piano, causing waterfalls and fountains of beautiful melodies to spill into every corner of the room, were spinning crochet mats as fine as spiders' webs to sit under porcelain figurines of shepherdesses, and young men in striped waistcoats and white wigs. Mrs Strauss had lived in Israel since 1934, when she and her husband had fled from Germany, but her Hebrew was still very foreign-sounding.

'Please to call me Madame,' she had said, when Daskeh first went to her for lessons. 'This is what I am used to.'

Daskeh went into the room Madame called 'The Salon'. Mrs Strauss said: 'In one minute, I will be all for you, Daskeh. First I will go into the kitchen for the cold drink jug. A person can faint today, it is so hot. Please to meet my son, Alex. Alex, please to meet my pupil, Daskeh.'

The salon was very dark, because the shutters were closed to keep out the sun. Daskeh could just see, though, the shape of a young man sitting on the hard, uncomfortable sofa. He stood up when his name was spoken.

'Hello,' he said. 'Come and sit down. This is the only room that's not like an oven. My mother will bring home-made lemonade, which is delicious.'

Daskeh forgot her shyness at once. 'I've heard such a lot about you . . . how you were the most gifted violinist for your age, playing in concerts when you were six, or was it five?'

Alex laughed. 'You know how parents exaggerate. I don't think I was ever that good, and in any case . . . well, it doesn't matter. How about you? How long have you been learning piano?'

'About four years.'

'And are you good?'

'Not very good,' said Daskeh, 'but I like it. I especially like hearing Madame . . . I mean your mother . . . play the pieces for me. That's the best bit.'

It occurred to Daskeh as she spoke that Madame had been very quiet on the subject of her son for a very long time now. She tried to remember when was the last time she had heard something about him, and couldn't really bring it to mind. She said: 'I think I thought you'd gone to Europe or something. I can't really recall.'

Alex laughed. 'Not Europe. I've been in hospital. In fact, I live in Tel-Aviv. I'm visiting my mother now. Convalescing.'

'Were you ill?' Daskeh peered through the gloom at him. He looked strong enough from what she could see.

'No, not ill. I was injured during the war. My arms . . . they were badly burned, so I've been in hospital, having treatment. Of course, my hands and arms are not a pretty sight, but at least I still have them. My hands, I mean. And, more importantly, I'm alive.'

At that moment, Mrs Strauss called Daskeh for her lesson.

'I have to go now,' she said. 'It was lovely to meet you.'

'I'm sure we'll meet again soon,' said Alex. 'I'm usually here in the afternoons.'

'Daskeh! You are not concentrating! What has happened to your scales? Do you have fingers or do you have instead sausages? Quick and delicate, please remember. Quick and delicate.'

Daskeh took her hands off the keys, and turned to Mrs Strauss. She was struggling not to cry, but in spite of all her efforts, two tears were trickling down her cheeks, towards her chin. She wiped them away with the backs of her hands.

'Child! Child! What have I said?' Mrs Strauss was fluttery with remorse. 'Please, not to cry on account of the clumsy scale. Please!'

'It's not the scales, Madame. It's Alex. I spoke to Alex in the salon, and I can't stop thinking about it – his. hands. I look at my fingers and I see his, and I can't bear to think of it. You used to tell such stories of him playing the violin. I'm sorry, Madame. I'll stop now and we can go on with the lesson.'

Mrs Strauss had stiffened. Her fingers (magic fingers) were clenched into two small fists on the mauve fabric of her dress. She hung her head and spoke in such a low voice that Daskeh had to lean forward to hear what she was saying: 'Every day I thank God he's alive, every day. What matters it, not being able to play the violin when there are young men like him dead and under the earth? What matters? Even his hands he still has, and his legs. Have you seen them near the hospital with no legs sometimes . . . and no arms. I cannot look at them. Alex is lucky. So I tell myself.' Mrs Strauss looked up. Tears were running down her cheeks and she did nothing to stop them. She said to Daskeh:

'But it *does* matter, does it not? Every single tiny thing matters . . . everything that is spoiled, made ugly, broken by war. And even for good causes, for good reasons, people are still hurt. In big ways and small ways. People are hurt and some get better altogether, and some get a little bit better, but nothing stays how it was.' Mrs Strauss shook her head and stood up.

'I go now to wash my face, child. I am glad to have a son who is alive. I am crying for other mothers not so fortunate. You will play B flat minor with both hands. Two octaves, till I return. I will listen from the bathroom.'

Daskeh's fingers found the notes. Mechanically, she played the scale up and down the piano, again and again without seeing the keys at all. She saw Alex sitting in the darkened salon, and Danny dreaming of the metal skeletons of trucks burning on a dusty hillside.

The following week, Daskeh persuaded Danny to

go with her to music.

'It's pointless lying on your bed and moping,' she'd said. 'Walk with me. Look at all the shops. It'll take your mind off – well, off your troubles. And you need some air. You look awful.'

That was true. Danny had purple smudges under his eyes from not sleeping, and his thin, white face was thinner and whiter than usual. Daskeh had told him about Alex.

'He's Madame's son. He's very nice and he used to be a real soldier. He's hurt his hands and is staying with his mother till he's better.'

'I don't want to meet him,' said Danny. 'What makes you think I want to see a real soldier? I'd be embarrassed, because I'm such a coward, I'm even frightened of my dreams.'

'Oh, for Heaven's sake, Danny!' said Daskeh. 'Just come to music. Let your life be normal at least when you're not sleeping! And I'll buy you a doughnut. You look as if you could use one, too, I can tell you. Skinny as a rake!' She smiled, and Danny agreed to go.

'Your stomach-ache is better, I see,' said Mrs Strauss to Danny. 'I am very pleased. Come, we will go straight in to the piano, and after your lesson, I will put you in the salon to wait for Daskeh, and you will have some of my strudel.'

Danny opened his mouth to tell Mrs Strauss he'd just had a doughnut, and then closed it again. He knew that when Mrs Strauss decided her pupils should take some refreshment, they were well advised not to argue.

'Is Alex here?' said Daskeh.

'He has gone for a walk,' said Mrs Strauss. 'Later, perhaps he will be here.'

Danny went into his lesson feeling relieved. He knew Daskeh would be disappointed. He couldn't imagine why she wanted him to meet this Alex so much. Whatever would he, Danny, have to say to someone who had been heroic enough to be injured in battle? He sat on the piano stool and tried to concentrate on arpeggios. Music was comforting. Music was safe.

After his lesson, Danny sat in the salon, washing bites of apple strudel down with iced lemonade, and listening to Daskeh playing her Mozart. Apart from the music, which sounded ghostly and distant through the closed door, there was nothing but silence all around him. He could hear no voices from the street, no traffic noises, no wirelesses playing in other apartments. The heat pressed down on his head, like an iron, even in this room that had been darkened to keep it cool. Danny felt exhaustion pulling him down, dragging at all his limbs, weighing on his eyelids. He closed his eyes. Just for a second, he thought sleepily. I'll open them soon. Very soon. Somewhere, a door banged and Danny's eyes flew open. He shook himself a little to make sure he was properly awake.

'Hello!' said a tall young man, coming into the room. 'You must be Danny.'

'Yes,' said Danny. 'I am. But how do you know?'

'Well, I'm Alex, Mrs Strauss's son and she told

me that you and Daskeh were coming today. I remember Daskeh from last week. You were ill, I think. You had a stomach-ache, but I can see you're better because you've eaten some of my mother's strudel.' The young man flung himself on to the sofa, which looked as though it were too small to hold him. He grinned at Danny. 'Aren't I a good detective?'

'No,' said Danny, grinning back. 'I never did have a stomach-ache. That was just what Daskeh told your mother.'

Alex sat up straight. 'Aha! The mystery deepens! Why should someone *without* a stomach-ache pretend that he is someone *with* a stomach-ache? Don't tell me. Let me guess. You hadn't done enough practice on your scales and you were terrified that my mother would smack you across the fingers with a ruler!'

Danny burst out laughing. 'No, no, Madame never hits us. That's not the reason. The reason is,' Danny hesitated. 'I didn't want to say what was *really* the matter with me. It was . . . silly. Embarrassing.'

'Honestly? Then let me guess again. I'm looking for embarrassing ailments. A boil on your bottom that prevented you from sitting on a piano stool? No? A bad attack of smelly feet? No? You woke up and found that your fingers had turned into pickled cucumbers? No? I give up. You'll have to tell me.'

'I can't.'

'But you must, otherwise curiosity will make me explode.'

'You'll laugh.'

'Will you tell me if I promise not to laugh?'

'All right,' Danny said, and immediately thought: why am I going to tell him? I *want* to tell him. I want to tell him everything. Why?

'I'm ready,' said Alex. 'Don't keep me in suspense. I promise I won't laugh, however funny it is.'

I'll say it very quickly, Danny thought, and then it'll all be over.

'I have bad dreams. I hate them so much that I try not to sleep, and then I get tired. That's all. I'm sorry.'

Alex didn't laugh. He didn't even smile. He sat frozen, like a statue, looking straight in front of him, and not seeing anything. Danny didn't know what to do. What had happened? Was Alex teasing him? What should he say? Should he say anything? The silence grew and grew and filled the shadowy room. After what seemed like minutes, Alex turned to look at him.

'Danny, don't be sorry.' He stood up and walked over to the window. 'What you've been going through is much worse than any stomach-ache. I don't think it's embarrassing or silly at all. In fact, I know it isn't.'

'You know?' Danny felt bewildered. Alex came back to the sofa and sat down heavily. He looked at Danny and smiled.

'I have the most terrible dreams, Danny. Do you see these hands?' He held up two bandaged hands. 'I won't take the bandages off. There's nothing very pleasant under them, I can tell you that, but it's beautiful compared with what I have to look at while I sleep. I was burned, you see. And some of my friends . . . well, they would have been very pleased to have escaped with injured hands. So I try to console myself. I try to tell myself that the dreams will fade. That the memories will get paler and paler as time goes on. My doctors tell me that is what will happen. But it's bad, isn't it, while it lasts? Quite bad enough to make you miss a piano lesson. Tell me what you dream about.'

'Bab-el-Waad,' said Danny. 'I dream I'm in a truck that's on fire and the fire is getting nearer and nearer and it's going to be all around me in a minute, so I have to wake up.'

'That sounds very like my dreams,' Alex said. 'Except in mine, I have to go into a burning room, in a burning house, to bring somebody out, and I never know who it is I'm trying to save, because I can never find them.' Alex's voice faded to silence.

'I thought,' Danny whispered, 'that I was stupid. Cowardly, to be scared of dreaming about such things. I didn't know that soldiers have bad dreams too.'

Alex laughed. 'Soldiers have worse dreams than anyone else, because they see and do worse things than almost anybody else. If they didn't have dreams, they would be machines and not people.'

'Daskeh's father,' said Danny, 'told her that if you have a nightmare and you talked about it to someone, that made it better. Do you think that's true?'

Alex said: 'I feel better. Don't you? Just talking to you has made me feel more cheerful. How about you?'

'I'm relieved,' Danny said. 'I thought it was me. Just me. But I wish . . .'

'What? What do you wish?'

'I wish Bab-el-Waad could be cleared up. I wish they'd take all the metal skeletons and bury them. Get rid of them, so that no one needs to see them any more and get bad dreams from thinking about them.'

'No,' said Alex. 'It's important that people should see it. As often as they can bear to look. It's important that everyone remembers exactly what it is that war can do, and what war looks like. It might prevent them from fighting again. It might teach them to search more carefully for peace.'

Danny said: 'Yes. Yes, I suppose you're right.' He smiled at Alex. 'Do you think I could have another piece of strudel? Suddenly, I'm hungry.'

'Certainly,' said Alex. 'Please do. And I'll have a bit as well. I'm also hungry.'

They sat and munched quietly in the salon, and Daskeh's music came to them from behind the door of the next room, falling around them like a cooling mist, like a blessing.

CARDBOARD BOXES FULL OF AMERICA 1954

'I can guess what happened to Danny,' said Harry. 'He was killed in some war, and that awful nightmare of his came true. I bet that's what happened.'

'You couldn't be more wrong,' said Aunt Rachel. 'He is still very much alive, and what's more, he's now a very high-ranking officer in the Army. So there you are. You can never guess how human beings will turn out. That's one thing I've learned in my life, and there is no shortage of wars for people to be brave in. I wish it wasn't the case, but it is, certainly in this part of the world.'

Harry knelt down on the carpet again.

'Who's this?' he asked, looking at a picture of a skinny girl with long plaits.

'That's another great-niece of mine, Reuben's granddaughter, Malka. She was born when I was nearly eighteen.'

'I know Malka! She lives in Chicago. She came and visited us once. She has the reddest hair and the bluest eyes I ever saw. You can't see that in this picture.'

'She was bound to end up in America, because of the parcels.'

'What parcels?'

'Listen to the story, and you'll find out.'

*　　*　　*

Whenever Malka looked out of the dining-room window, she was hoping for a glimpse of Aviva Masner in the apartment across the street. Sometimes at night, the Masners forgot to draw their curtains, and the full glory of the lighted room beyond the glass could be seen as clearly as if it were a stage in a theatre, brightly lit and waiting for the actors. The furniture was modern – so modern that Malka felt she recognized it from some shop-window or other. The wood was pale and yellowish, and the upholstery was striped. The walls were full of pictures that were also modern: ladies with eyes and noses in strange places, and paintings of houses with animals floating in the sky above them. There was a lace mat on the dining-room table with a cut-glass vase on it. The Sabbath candlesticks (which Malka only ever saw on a Friday evening when they were on the table) were made of silver, elaborately decorated. The Masners were rich, that was clear, and they not only *were* rich, they looked it. Dr Masner was a dentist and wore dark suits and very shiny shoes. Mrs Masner had a permanent wave put into her hair every few weeks by Shulamith, the chief hairdresser at Chez Yolande on Allenby Road. This Malka knew because Shulamith was one of her mother's friends. She (Mrs Masner) wore dresses all the time, and Malka had never seen her in an apron. Perhaps she

194

wore one in the kitchen and was careful to take it off before she came into the dining-room, or perhaps (Malka liked this version the best) the Masners had a servant who spent her days slaving away over a hot stove, or working her fingers to the bone, and who was only allowed into the grander rooms in order to clean and polish and dust.

Even the Masner apartment, however, was not splendid enough for Aviva Masner. Malka had never seen a real princess, but she was sure that Aviva looked like one. She had two long, blonde plaits hanging down her back, and these plaits were always smooth and shiny, and never had any straggling hairs escaping from them. Her brow was wide and pale, in spite of playing in the sun, and her eyes were blue. Malka had blue eyes too, but they were washed-out looking and sometimes greenish and her eyelashes and eyebrows were red, just like her wild, curling hair. Aviva's eyes were like a summer sky and her eyelashes were thick and quite dark. She was beautiful. Everybody in Malka's apartment block and in Aviva's own building wanted to be her friend. When the girls gathered in the yard behind Malka's building to play, there was fierce competition to be Aviva's partner, to lend her a skipping rope, to be chosen for her team. Dafna, Maya, Hannah and especially Nurit were Malka's best friends, but she hadn't seen very much of them lately. She had been too busy trying to get into Aviva's gang.

'Why don't you walk to school with Nurit any more?' Malka's mother asked.

'She goes too early,' Malka answered. 'I'd rather wait and go later.'

The truth was, if she went later, she could time it carefully and bump into Aviva as she came out of her building, and if Irit, Liora and Ronit weren't with her then she, Malka, would be allowed to walk along beside her all the way to school. It was true that Aviva never spoke in a very interesting way. She wasn't nearly as much fun as Nurit. In fact, she had a habit of not listening properly, and of not looking at you but at a spot two inches above your head, as if there were someone more important standing just behind you. Malka forgave her, though, because she had such perfectly ironed blouses and such extremely white ankle socks and her sandals – every day! – looked as if they'd come out of the box from the shoeshop that very second. Nurit was always waiting for Malka at school, by the gate.

'I don't know how you can bear to walk with that Aviva,' she said. 'She's boring and stuck-up.'

'She's not boring,' Malka said. 'It's just that I don't know her well enough. She's quite shy. I'm sure she's fascinating when you get to know her. Everyone wants to be friends with her, to be one of her gang. I'm not the only one.'

'I don't want to,' said Nurit. 'So there. Anyway, you've been walking to school with her for ages, and you've been sucking up to her in the playground, and it still hasn't worked, has it? You're still not in her gang, are you?'

'I do not suck up to her!'

'You do.'

'I do not.'

'Oh, come on, let's go in now. I'm fed up with talking about Aviva.'

Malka followed Nurit into the classroom. Aviva sat far away from them, next to the window. At home, she was forced to play with children from nearby buildings who all used the same yard, but at school she went about with the girls who lived in big houses in Rehavia, and pretended she hardly knew her own neighbours, apart from Irit, Liora and Ronit of course, who were, thought Malka, like Aviva's ladies-in-waiting.

One morning, towards the end of the long summer holidays, a small yellow card arrived in the post.

'Look, Malka!' said her mother. 'There's another parcel waiting for us at the Post Office. A parcel from America!'

Malka said: 'When can we go and get it? Can we go today? Can we go now? Or this afternoon? I can't bear to wait for it, not even for a second.'

'We'll go this afternoon,' said Malka's mother, trying to sound grown-up and organized. Malka knew that her mother was almost as excited as she was herself. There was nothing in the world as wonderful as a parcel from America. Malka, since she was a baby, thought of America as a Paradise full of beautiful things, like the oilcloth on the dining-room table, the tall tea-glasses with red and blue flowers painted on them, and the shiny white handbag with a clasp that looked like a gold butterfly. Whenever anyone asked, 'Where did you get such a treasure?' the answer would always come flying back: 'From our sisters in America!'

When she was small, Malka imagined the whole of America to be a huge shop, a kind of department store, and she pictured her aunts walking along between the counters, choosing delightful items to put in cardboard boxes. As she grew older and began to go to the Zion Cinema with Nurit and Maya on Friday afternoons before the arrival of the Sabbath, she saw other pictures of America. It was a big country, she knew from her lessons, and she could see that it needed to be if it was to contain ranches with cowboys and lots of cows and horses in them, and little dusty Western towns and mountains (also full of cowboys) and cities crowded with tall grey buildings called skyscrapers, full of men in suits and ties and ladies in high-heeled shoes and dresses with skirts that stuck out and round white collars. There were also films in which an actress called Esther Williams did a lot of swimming, and those had tropical beaches in them, and some films were about long ago and had ladies in crinolines swishing all over the place, but they all filled the screen with bright colours and music and movement, and they packed Malka's head with glorious pictures. Now she imagined her aunts and uncles worked in offices and lived in homes like those favoured by Doris Day, and she and Nurit used to cut out photographs of film stars from every newspaper and magazine they could find and stick them in big scrapbooks.

Malka thought about her scrapbooks while she waited for the morning to pass, waiting for the time to come when the parcel could be collected. Earlier, Nurit had called to see if Malka wanted to go to the zoo.

'I'm going with my mother to fetch a parcel from the Post Office. And besides, we've seen the animals hundreds of times.'

'I don't care,' Nurit answered. 'I like them. I like them better than I like some people. But another parcel from America! You are lucky. I wish we could get one.'

At last, the clock crept round to the afternoon, and it was time to set out.

'We'll take the bus,' said Malka's mother, 'because otherwise the sun will flatten us both. And of course we'll have to take a bus back, because the parcel will be too heavy to carry through the streets.'

Malka hated buses. As soon as the doors opened, everyone who was waiting pushed to get on. There was always someone carrying something bulky or difficult. Once, it was an old woman holding five live chickens by their yellow legs as if they were a bunch of squawking flowers. Today, Malka thought, on the way back it'll be us, trying to hold the parcel on our laps, if we're lucky enough to get a seat. Often you had to stand. I wish I were a grown-up, Malka thought, then I wouldn't have to look at so many belts and waistcoat pockets and corseted bottoms. I bet the Masners never have to ride on buses. I bet they take taxis everywhere.

'Lovely! Seats for both of us!' said Malka's mother. 'We can ride like two queens in our carriage.'

Malka looked out of the window. There was the Zion Cinema, Café Vienna, and all the little shops she liked to look at, the ones full of jewellery and silver and copper knick-knacks. There were the kiosks selling fizzy red drinks that tickled your nose, and there was the man who pushed a huge pot of boiling water along the street on a trolley. He'd cooked corn on the cob in this pot and you could stop him and buy some. He used to plunge a long fork into the water and bring out the corn as if he were spearing a golden fish. Then he presented it to you like a gift, wrapped in some of its own pale green leaves. The smell came to Malka through the window of the bus and made her feel hungry.

At the Post Office, they had to wait in a queue, and when their turn came, Malka held her breath while the man behind the metal grille looked along a whole shelf of parcels to see which one was theirs. Perhaps it was lost, perhaps it had been given to someone else by mistake, perhaps they would have to go home without it for some reason. Malka looked at the packages and tried to guess which one it could be. She did this every time a parcel arrived and she had never once chosen the right one. When the man (oh, at long last!) found theirs, it was always bigger, more splendid, more enticing than Malka had imagined.

'It's a miracle,' said the Post Office man from under his bushy black moustache 'that's there's any of America left to send . . . so many people shipping pieces of it over the sea in cardboard boxes!' He waved his hand at the mountain of brown parcels behind him. 'That's all I see all day – cardboard boxes full of America!'

That evening, summoned by telephone, the female members of the family gathered to divide the spoils.

'The men pretend they aren't interested in such things,' said Malka's mother 'but they're very happy to wear smart American suits and drink American coffee from tins.'

Malka sat and watched as wonder after wonder emerged from the opened box: dresses in colours and patterns you dream about, blouses with embroidery down the front and buttons like pearls, tins of coffee and dishcloths and teatowels and gadgets like potato peelers and tea strainers, and beads made out of plastic that looked, everyone agreed, 'just exactly like moonstones.' There were shoes for babies with little rabbits or birds on them, modern shirts for the men with checks and stripes all over them, and everything came in all sorts of sizes to fit almost the whole family. For the children, there were always packets of raisins and shocking pink bubble gum stuck into the corners, and also chocolate bars in vividly-coloured wrappers. Distributing the contents of the parcel took ages, and Malka wished it could take even longer. Every item was debated, discussed, argued over.

'Will it fit Naomi?'

'Well, if not, Rifka can try it. Or Shoshanna.'

'Is this shirt too big for Chaim?'

'He had a shirt last time. It's Nathan's turn.'

On and on, the talk would go, round and round above Malka's head, and she only half-heard it. She was too busy looking, touching, stroking and above all, sniffing everything that came out of the box. It smelled different. It smelled particularly American, especially the comic books which she sometimes found, tucked in the folds of sheets or towels whose fluffiness had been flattened by weeks of lying in a parcel.

At last, everything had been taken out and its ownership decided upon. Tea was being made in the kitchen. Malka looked into the empty box.

'Hey!' she said, 'you've missed this. It's a scarf.'

A few cousins looked up and Aunt Pnina said: 'You can keep it, Malka, I'm sure. There wasn't such a lot for you this time. No one will mind.'

And it was true. Everyone was too busy cuddling her own treasures to worry about one scarf. Malka spread it on the table in front of her.

'You can see through it,' she told Aunt Pnina. 'Look, it's like a kind of mist.'

'It's chiffon,' said Aunt Pnina.

'I think it's nylon,' said a knowledgeable modern cousin called Ilana.

'It's so pretty,' said Malka, 'whatever it is. I love it.'

'Wear it in good health,' said Malka's mother, who was setting the teacups out on the table.

Malka hung the scarf on the chair near her bed that night. The background was yellowy-beige and on it were printed big flowers with pink and red and orange petals and spiky green leaves. Tomorrow, Malka thought, I'll wear it round my neck in the yard. That will show Aviva that she's not the only one with beautiful clothes.

The next day, Nurit and Malka had just finished chalking a grid on the asphalt, ready for hopscotch, when Aviva came into the yard with Irit, Liora and Ronit. Malka looked up and smiled.

'Hello, Aviva. Would you like to play hopscotch?'

'No – no, we're not staying very long.' She looked at Malka with more attention than she'd ever shown before. 'That's a nice scarf,' she said.

'She's like a magpie,' Nurit muttered under her breath. 'She always has a beady eye open for treasures.'

'Ssh!' said Malka to Nurit. To Aviva she said: 'Thank you. It came in a parcel from America.' She couldn't resist boasting a little. 'We often get parcels from America. We've got lots of relatives who live there.'

'Really?' Aviva looked quite impressed. 'You are lucky.' She paused for a moment, and then she said: 'It's too hot to be outside. We're going to play in my house. 'Bye.' Then she turned and walked out of the yard, followed by her friends.

'The hopscotch grid is ready,' said Nurit, who had continued to mark it out while Malka talked to Aviva. Malka sighed. She and Nurit hopped about half-heartedly for a while. All Malka could think about was Aviva and her friends, probably drinking iced lemonade at this very moment, up in

the cool apartment. She longed to be inside with them, one of Aviva's gang, maybe even her very best friend.

'I'm going home now,' she said to Nurit. 'It's too hot to hop. Do you want to come?'

'I've got to go and get some bread for my mother. Then we're going out somewhere. Will I see you tomorrow?'

'I expect so,' said Malka, and added: 'Maybe,' because an idea had just flashed into her mind. It was such a marvellous idea that for a few moments she couldn't quite believe she'd been so clever. Oh, it was wonderful! Aviva would never be able to resist . . . but should Malka wait until she saw Aviva in the yard, or should she go up and knock at her door? She would have to talk to Aviva, and how could she do that without nearly melting with embarrassment? She needed a way of talking without being seen. She needed something like a telephone. As soon as this notion came to her, Malka said to herself: why not the telephone? I can look in the book and find the number. Dr Masner is sure to be in if he's a dentist. But what will I say? How will I put it? Will I dare to talk at all?

When she reached home, Malka looked up the Masners' number and wrote it down on a piece of paper which she put in her pocket. She thought about telephoning all through the afternoon, and then at last, while her mother was busy in the kitchen preparing supper and making a lot of clatter with dishes and pans, Malka decided to do it. She dialled the number, and then she heard the ringing tone and imagined the phone in the Masners' apartment filling the room with its loud cries. Then someone said:

'Jerusalem 26385,' and Malka said:

'I'd like to speak to Aviva, please.'

'This is Aviva speaking. Who's that?'

'It's Malka. From across the road.'

'Oh.'

'I'd like to ask you something.'

'Go on, then.' (She sounded impatient, Malka thought.)

'I wanted to know if you like my scarf.'

'I told you I did. I think it's lovely. What a stupid thing to ring about.' (Malka thought: now she seems cross.)

'I wanted to ask you if you'd like it as a present.'

Silence, then: 'You want to give me your scarf?'

'Yes.'

'Why?'

'No reason. I just want you to have it. Perhaps I could play with you and Irit and Liora and Ronit sometimes.' (Did that sound casual enough? Malka wondered.)

'Aah, I see. If you give me your scarf, I've got to let you be in our gang. Is that it?'

Malka blushed and felt happy that at least Aviva couldn't see her. Oh, well, she thought, what have I got to lose? She said: 'Yes, that's it.'

A very long silence followed. Malka, straining her ears, could hear whispering. Obviously, Aviva was consulting the other members of the gang. It went on for ages. At long last, Aviva came back on the line and said:

'Hello, Malka? Are you still there?'

'Yes.'

'It's O.K. We've decided that you can be in our gang. Bring the scarf to my apartment tomorrow at ten.'

'Thank you, Aviva. Yes, I will. Goodbye.'

She put the telephone back on its cradle and hugged herself with sheer pleasure. She was one of Aviva's gang now, a properly invited member. From tomorrow she would be one of the ladies-in-waiting.

Two weeks after what Malka thought of as 'The day of the telephone call' she walked up to the third floor of her apartment building and knocked on the door of Nurit's flat.

Nurit opened the door, looked puzzled for a moment when she saw Malka, then her face cleared and she smiled.

'Hello, Malka. I haven't seen you for ages.'

'I know, I'm sorry. Can I come in?'

'O.K. Come into my room. Is Aviva busy? Why aren't you playing with her? I thought you were her friend now.'

'I'm your friend too,' said Malka. 'I've always been your friend, ever since we were babies.'

'But you've stopped coming to play . . . so I don't know if you're my friend any more.'

'Of course I'm your friend,' said Malka. 'I'm sorry I haven't been coming to your house so often.'

'You've been busy. Has she got bored with you?'

'No,' said Malka. 'I've got bored with her. She's not very nice, Nurit.'

'I knew that. I could see she wasn't.'

'How did you know? She's so beautiful, and she has such lovely clothes.'

'That,' said Nurit, 'isn't enough to make her nice.'

'No, but I wanted to be her friend. I wanted to be asked into her lovely apartment.'

'Is it lovely?'

'I suppose it is. But you can't make even the smallest mess. If you eat a biscuit, Mrs Masner comes up behind you with a dustpan and brush, and those girls never do anything. They just play dressing-up and dolls. They don't go anywhere except the yard. They never go to the zoo or the cinema. They've never heard of all our film stars.'

'What sort of games do they play with their dolls?'

'Hospitals, mostly. They were playing that this morning when it happened . . .' Malka's voice faded to silence.

'When what happened?' asked Nurit. Malka looked up.

'Do you remember the scarf? The one that came from the last American parcel?'

'The one you gave Aviva,' said Nurit. 'I remember it. It was lovely.'

'I *loved* that scarf,' said Malka. 'I dreamed about it at night after I'd given it away. Well, Aviva stopped wearing it round her neck after a couple of days and I thought she must have hung it up with her best dresses, or folded it neatly in one of her drawers. Well, yesterday when we were playing hospitals, she needed a bandage, so she rummaged round in a big basket full of bits of duster and old rags, and then out came the American scarf. I recognized it even though it was crumpled and dirty. "This'll do for a bandage," Aviva said and she began to wrap it round the cut knee of one of her silly dolls. Irit and Liora and Ronit laughed and I know they were really laughing at me. I wanted to hit Aviva, but I didn't dare. I wanted to tear the scarf off the doll's knee and wash it and iron it, but it was spoiled now and I didn't really like it any more. So I just said I had to go home and I came here. I won't play with her again. She's horrible.'

Nurit nodded. 'There's a lovely film at the Zion

this week. It's called "By the light of the silvery moon", and it's got Doris Day in it.'

'Lovely!' said Malka and smiled at Nurit. The next time there was an American parcel, she decided, Nurit would get something from it. It would be a present suitable for a proper best friend: a little piece of America.

'Did Aviva get her come-uppance?' said Harry.

'No,' said Aunt Rachel. 'She went on just as she always had. I still see her sometimes. She's less beautiful now. In fact, she looks much as her mother used to look.

'Tomorrow morning I'll take you for a walk, to see the places I've told you about. Go and sit on the balcony now and I'll make us a cup of fresh tea.' She went into the kitchen.

Harry sat on the balcony, shivering a little in the chilly night. He thought of Pnina, and Miriam and Daskeh and Danny and Malka and how they had all been children long ago, walking about in Jerusalem, just as he was going to walk tomorrow. Directly across from Aunt Rachel's apartment, the high façade of a hotel reached into the sky. People were turning lights on now and everywhere he looked Harry could see them: golden windows shining in the blue night like small, rectangular stars.